A Bite Of Yummy

Finding Life at the Table

- Lisa M. Jacobs -

PLAIN JOINTS ADAPTED TO THE TABLE OF THE WEALTHY AS WELL AS MY TABLE AT HOME.

As hardly any dinner is properly served without a simple joint, which may be deposited either on the table or sideboard, I have placed all plain joints, as also the directions for choosing meat, at the commencement of My Kitchen at Home, to which I shall beg to refer my readers while making the bills of fare, or choosing different qualities of meat.

OF THE CHOOSING AND ROASTING OF PLAIN JOINTS.

Here I must claim all the attention of my readers: many of the profession will, I have no doubt, be surprised that I should dwell upon a subject which appears of so little importance, saying that, from the plain cook to the most professed, all know how to roast or boil a piece of meat, but there I must beg their pardon; I will instance myself: for, previously to my forming any intention of writing the present work, I had not devoted the time necessary to become professionally acquainted with it, always depending upon my roasting cook, who had constant practice, myself only having the knowledge of whether or not properly done. I have since not only studied it closely, but have made in many respects improvements upon the old system, and many discoveries in that branch which I am sure is the most beneficial to all classes of society (remembering, as I have before stated, that three parts of the animal food of this country is served either plain roasted or boiled). My first study was the fire, which I soon perceived was too deep, consumed too much coal, and required poking every half hour, thus sending dust and dirt all over the joints, which were immediately basted to wash it off; seeing plainly this inconvenience, I immediately remedied it by inventing my new roasting fire-place (see page 622), by which means I saved two hundred-weight of coals per day, besides the advantage of never requiring to be poked, being narrow and perpendicular; the fire is lighted with the greatest facility, and the front of the fire being placed a foot back in the chimney-piece, throws the heat of the fire direct upon the meat, and not out at the sides, as many persons know from the old roasting ranges. I have many times placed ladies or gentlemen, visiting the club, within two feet of the fire when six large joints have been roasting, and they have been in perfect ignorance that it was near them until upon opening the wing of the screen (see same Plate) by surprise, they have appeared quite terrified to think they were so near such an immense furnace. My next idea was to discontinue basting, perhaps a bold attempt to change and upset at once the custom of almost all nations and ages, but being so confident of its evil effects and tediousness, I at once did away with it, and derived the greatest benefit (for explanation, see remarks at the commencement of the roasts in the Kitchen of the Wealthy), for the quality of meat in England is, I may say, superior to any other nation; its moist soil producing fine grass almost all the year round, which is the best food for every description of cattle, whilst in some countries not so favoured by nature they are obliged to have recourse to artificial food, which fattens the animals, but decreases the flavour of the meat; and, again, we must take into consideration the care and attention paid by the farmers and graziers to improve the stock of those unfortunate benefactors of the human family.

Every country is famous, more or less, for some produce, so is every county; for instance, for the best beef we are indebted principally to Scotland: the Highland ox, which if bred in Scotland, kept there until four years old, and fed twelve months in Norfolk, cannot be surpassed; those also that are killed in Scotland are likewise very commendable, but the connoisseur would give the preference by far to those that had undergone a change of atmosphere and pasturage. Norfolk also produces excellent beef, as likewise does Herefordshire, which three sorts are ranked as the best by the first judges.

The Brighton downs are noted for producing sheep of the first quality, next to which may be ranked those of the Norfolk downs, they are rather larger, more fleshy, and the meat sometimes a darker colour. Herefordshire also produces some very excellent. The Scotch mutton is also very good, and deservedly of high repute, but I rarely ever use it, as it is killed in Scotland and hurriedly packed, which causes it not to look so well, and frequently very much bruises it; but those of Leicestershire are, in my opinion, quite the contrary, being coarse meat and very fat; I consider it unworthy of making its appearance upon the table of a man of wealth. When residing at Melton Mowbray I tried several haunches, even after hanging a month in winter, and then roasted to perfection, I could not find in them any flavour worthy of the taste of an epicure; I consider it more as a useful nourishment than a delicate meat.

The best Welsh mutton is brought direct from its native mountains, the heath upon which it feeds gives a very rich flavour to the meat, which is very dark without much fat; many are fed in some of the English counties, they are very excellent and much fatter, but do not possess the same wild flavour.

The beat veal to be obtained in the spring time of the year comes from the west of England, being rather small and very white, but there is a steady supply of good veal from Surrey and Essex throughout the year. Although very fine veal may be obtained in this country, it is not to be compared to the quality of veal we obtain in France; the veal of Pontoise, a little town six miles from Paris, outrivals any; I would venture to say that one pound of that veal would make a better stock than double the quantity of the veal procured here: no one can account for it, but such is the actual case; although there the quality of any other description of animal food is deficient, we have to boast of the excellent flavour, succulence, and excessive whiteness of our veal.

House lamb may be obtained throughout the whole year, but there is no great demand for it before February; grass lamb makes its appearance now much earlier than formerly: the quality much depends upon the winter season; if a mild winter they may really be fed upon grass, but if the contrary, they must be fed with prepared food, which increases their size but diminishes their quality.

Pork for roasting is best when about six months old, Berkshire and Hampshire producing the best. The size of a leg of pork should not exceed more than seven pounds, nor much less than six. I do not know why, but of late years pork has lost in a great measure its popularity, and but seldom appears upon a nobleman's table; it is in season from October to about March.

No. 1. *Sirloin of Beef.* The royal honour which this bold and handsome dish received from the merry monarch, who conferred upon it the honour of knighthood, good Sir Loin, which title it has ever since retained (previously only bearing the cognomen of loin), and most likely will retain until the latest period: as a joint it claims precedence of all others. In roasting, the fillet and fat below keep the upper part moist, and when well roasted, such is the quantity of gravy, that after a few slices have been cut it may be taken from it with a spoon.

Procure a fine square piece of sirloin weighing about twenty pounds (which has been hung at least three weeks in winter, and eight or ten days, if possible, in summer, observing that the older the meat is the longer it will require keeping before cooking, and this remark applies to all kinds of meat, especially to beef and mutton), trim nicely, leaving the fat about an inch and a half in thickness over the fillet, cut a slice slantwise from the flap, which turn under, fixing it with skewers, thus giving the joint an oblong shape; with a sharp knife cut through the sinew (running along the chine-bones) in four or five places, or the meat would contract in roasting; make an incision in the centre of the chine-bones, lengthwise, with a chopper, through which pass a spit an inch wide and half an inch in thickness, bringing it out at the flap, keeping the centre, and avoiding the fillet. When the joint is larger it would be advisable to use a cradle-spit, which, however like the other spit, has its inconveniences, one making a hole through the meat, and the other pressing upon the fat, making it heavy; but in any kind of joint, if not over-roasted, you will never perceive the mark of the spit, as the cavity closes immediately upon the spit leaving it; always choose a spit corresponding to the size of the joint. In a large kitchen, where you require many joints roasting at one time, a cradle-spit is a nuisance, and must be used only where it cannot be avoided. Tie half a sheet of buttered foolscap paper upon each side of the beef, and place to roast, keeping it two feet from a very clear fire, let remain twenty minutes, then rub the top over with a piece of butter placed in the bowl of a large wooden spoon (see page 396), and place the beef back to the distance of three or four feet from the fire, allowing it two hours and a half to three hours to roast; take it from your spit, let remain a few minutes upon a dish until no more fat runs from it, when place it upon the dish you intend serving it on (previously taking out the piece of rump-bone affixed to the side to facilitate the carving; but in choosing a piece of sirloin obtain it if possible without any of that bone attached, or, at any rate, with but a very small piece, as the joint looks so much handsomer without it), pouring half a pint of good gravy (page 394) under; you will then perceive my object in not basting meat, the fat and the skin will be of a very light gold colour, which would have been quite the contrary if continually basted. By placing the meat too near the fire the fat quickly melts and falls into the dripping-pan, whilst by keeping it a tolerable distance it cooks gradually, and as the meat revolves runs over its surface, keeping it continually moist; and, again, by placing it too near the fire it is liable to catch, causing many persons to think that it has not been well basted; another evil in basting is, that by continually pouring hot fat over you cause that beautiful light fat attached to the joint to become heavy, and the gravy which invariably falls from the joint with the fat remains upon it, burns, and causes it to be very indigestible. It will also be easy to perceive in the habit of pouring a quantity of hot fat over all joints, that if three or four should be roasting together, one over the other, that one description of meat becomes basted with the fat and gravy of several, whilst the mere rubbing of a piece of butter over is not the least objectionable, as nothing can fall upon other joints but a little butter or clear fat, which cannot in the least interfere with the flavour of other meats, but still I would advise that lamb, veal, poultry, and even game, be kept at the top where there is beef, mutton, or pork roasting; this only applies to large establishments.

The above description is applied for the Kitchen of the Wealthy, but I must confess I do not object to a small piece of beef for my Kitchen at Home; I should proceed precisely as above, only procuring a piece of not more than eight, ten, or twelve pounds in weight; put a little water in the dripping-pan, place the beef upon a spit papered as before, put it very near the fire for a few minutes, rub over with butter, then put it back at the distance of two feet; let roast, if weighing from ten to twelve pounds, an hour and a half to two hours, depending much upon the fire, of which any person may judge with or without practice; take it up, dress upon your dish, then have the contents of your dripping-pan in a basin, from which extract the whole of the fat, and pour the gravy over the chine-bones, it will be very good, and save the trouble and expense of making gravy; a couple of Yorkshire puddings, of two eggs each, are very excellent cooked under the meat; before I had a smoke-jack in my small kitchen I used to roast very well with a bit of string. For the cottage kitchen, where there is no smoke-jack provided, you may roast very well with a piece of worsted or string, by hooking it to the meat, and then suspending it to a bracket fixed under the mantel-piece, which will enable you to remove it to any distance you think proper from the fire, making a tea-tray, at the distance of three feet from the fire, act as a screen; the bottle-jacks are not bad, but soon get out of repair.

No. 2. *Ribs of Beef.* A piece of from twenty to twenty-five pounds makes a very pretty joint; trim neatly by sawing off the tips of the chine-bones to make it stand flat, saw also about three inches from the tips of the ribs, merely sawing through the bones, which detach from the meat, leaving a flap, which fold under and fix with wooden skewers, not, however, pulling it too tight, or it would cause the skin to crack in roasting, which would produce a very bad effect; roast as directed for the sirloin, from two hours and a half to three hours would be sufficient, unless very thick. For a cold joint the ribs are better than the sirloin, which last should always be eaten hot.

At home I often have a piece of ribs of beef weighing from six to eight pounds, and roast by passing a very thin spit through, and placing it down before a moderate fire; or, if in a small cottage, hang it up with string as for the small sirloin; it would take from an hour and five minutes to an hour and a quarter roasting, being perpendicular you may baste it slightly, as it does not receive much nourishment from its own fat.

No. 3. *Rump of Beef.* This is also a very delicate joint, but can only be had to perfection in the winter months, as it requires hanging from three weeks to a month before it is in readiness to roast to perfection; procure one of from thirty to thirty-five pounds in weight, trim neatly, leaving all the fat, for, taking so long to roast, should it be short of fat it would go to table quite dry; roast it in a cradle-spit as directed for sirloin, but keeping it still further from the fire, and giving it from four hours and a half to five hours roasting, it might also be roasted in paste as directed for haunch of venison (No. 222), or wrap it up in several sheets of paper well buttered, and browned by taking off the paste twenty minutes before removing from the fire.

This bold joint never makes its appearance in my Kitchen at Home, but I have frequently used the piece of fillet attached to it, which weighs from three to five pounds; I leave about an inch of fat upon it, pass a small spit through, and roast from three quarters of an hour to an hour; for gravy I proceed as for the sirloin. Cold potatoes, previously boiled, put under it in the dripping-pan whilst roasting, and turned occasionally, are very excellent.

No. 4. *Baron of Beef.* It is an old saying that two extremes often meet, so with me, I leave my five pounds' joint roasting and, like Gulliver, make a step towards the empire of the giant. This is, indeed, a colossal joint, which at first sight would put a modest fire out of conceit, my smoke-jack out of order, and, above all, drive my few guests' appetites from their frugal stomachs; they not being initiated in the grandeur or importance of a civic or aristocratic banquet would consider it a mighty dish of vulgarity. But stay, friends, I would observe grandeur and magnitude are far from being vulgar; to prove that my assertion is correct I have the opinion of ages, for it is a dish almost as old as England herself. I have before stated that Charles the Second gave the title and importance to the sirloin, and I have no doubt the baron owes its origin also to some such cause or great event, which I will attempt to discover for the information of some of my readers who, like myself, at present may be entirely ignorant of its origin, which I feel assured will prove interesting.

A baron of beef is generally cut from a small ox, and includes the two rumps and two sirloins with one of the rib bones on each side; it must be trussed precisely as for a saddle of mutton; pass a spit, which of course must not be too large, through the spinal-marrow-bone, then wrap the beef up in paste as for a haunch of venison (No. 540), only a little thicker, add also more paper, set it three feet from a brisk fire, pouring fat over the paper to prevent its catching fire, twenty minutes afterwards remove the spit two feet farther from the fire, inclose it well with the fire-screen, and roast eight or nine hours, keeping it turned by hand; half an hour before it is done take off the paste and paper and give the beef a fine gold colour, when take up, dress in a dish with gravy under and serve. The ancient style was to serve a representation of St. George and the dragon, cut from vegetables, upon the top, fresh salad also of every description used to be placed around, but the whole was obliged to be removed at the commencement of carving.

Having promised my readers that I would make all possible inquiry relating to the origin of the inviting joint called baron of beef, a careful search into "Hone" and others, has not, I regret to say, been attended with quite a favorable result, and the only information which I can at present obtain is the legendary one that King John, after signing Magna Charta at Runnymede, partook of a repast in the company of his barons, consisting of the saddle and part of the ribs of beef roasted, and that hence arose the saying "baron of beef." Now this appears very much like the traveller's tale that had but one point in its favour, namely, that no one present could possibly contradict it.

No. 5. *Round of Beef.* "Here," says John Bull, with a good-humoured countenance (standing near a table upon which was a round of beef being prepared for dressing, clapping his hands upon his knees, and bending with no little difficulty his colossal stomach), "do you know, my excellent friend," says he to me, "I fear you cannot cook that glorious dish to perfection, for I have not yet forgotten your seven hours' dressing of a leg of mutton (p. 193), so if you are not above receiving a lesson I will give you one which will enable you to dress this all-important dish to perfection; for I prize it as I do my own roast beef of old England, and you must be aware that after the centuries of practice I have had that I must understand some little about it. Well, in the first place, the quality of the meat has a good deal to do with it, of which you have given a fair description, I therefore pass it over; but to proceed: it must be cut pretty freely from the knuckle and placed in a brine-tub, cover well with salt, rub it well in, leave it until the next day, when again rub it with the salt and brine created by the gravy from the meat, rubbing well every other day until it has remained a fortnight, that is, if of a good size, weighing from thirty to thirty-five pounds, if larger or smaller, more or less time, which must be left to your own good judgment, then take it out of the pickle, let drain twenty minutes, take out and form it of a good shape, folding the fat round, which fix with skewers, tying it round with a few yards of very wide tape, tie it up in a thin cloth, and place it in a large stock-pot with plenty of cold water, set upon a good fire and when beginning to boil draw it to the corner, where let simmer five hours, but two hours before it is done put in eight fine carrots, scraped and cut into six or eight pieces, twelve turnips (peeled), and two suet puddings, weighing from two and a half to three pounds each, these articles would, perhaps, cause the water to cease boiling, if so, place it again quite over the fire until it does boil; when done take out the round, let drain ten minutes, take it from the cloth, detach the tape, take out the skewers, replacing them as you take them out with long silver skewers, dress upon a large hot-water dish, and pour over about a quart of the liquor it was boiled in, cut a large slice from the top about two inches and a half in thickness, dress the carrots and turnips tastefully around and serve, with the puddings upon a separate dish, sending one after the other, they will eat much lighter. When upon the table it must be carved with a regular round-of-beef knife (very sharp) in slices not exceeding the thickness of half-a-crown piece, assisting each guest to a slice, also give one third fat, with a little of the carrot and turnip, but never dig the underdone part from the centre to oblige any one, for they that cannot eat from a joint well-cooked and fairly carved are not worthy of having one set before them. Some persons like them, when salted, to cut red quite through, I do not admire it, but it is done by adding two ounces of sal prunella and half a pound of saltpetre to every fifteen pounds of salt used in the pickling. When a round of beef is very large some persons place a tin tube in the centre to boil it, I do not think it a bad plan, as it causes it to cook more regular."

After receiving the above useful lesson, and being desirous of improving my profession in all its branches, I remembered that amongst the number of joints boiled to serve cold for large civic, agricultural, or benevolent anniversary dinners, the round of beef was the most prominent, and having seen it standing in dishes to get cold, with the dish filled with the gravy that runs from it, particularly if a little overdone, caused me to hit upon the following expedient to prevent the meat losing so much of its succulence: fill two large tubs with cold water, into which throw a few pounds of rough ice, and when the round is done throw it, cloth and all, into one of the tubs of ice water, let remain one minute, when take out and put it into the other tub, fill the first tub again with water, and continue the above process for about twenty minutes, then set it upon a dish, leaving the cloth on until the next day, or until quite cold; when opened the fat will be as white as possible, besides having saved the whole of the gravy. If no ice, spring water will answer the same purpose, but will require to be more frequently changed; the same mode would be equally successful with the aitch-bone.

The above is a joint which I have always considered too large for my Kitchen at Home, but the aitch-bone or brisket is easily managed.

No. 6. *Aitch-bone of Beef.* A good-sized one would weigh from fifteen to twenty pounds. Pickle it precisely as directed in the last, but one week would be sufficient, boil nearly three hours, and serve with the vegetables round as before, and a suet pudding separate; if for cold do not take the tape from it until cold, trim the top, run a silver skewer in at the extremity, and serve garnished with sprigs of very green fresh parsley.

No. 7. *Brisket of Beef.* The whole brisket would require pickling for a week, it must not be too fat; this being a long awkward joint may be cut in two, and served upon separate occasions, boil about five hours and serve as for the last two, with the vegetables around it; when upon table it must be cut into thin slices, fat and lean in fair proportions. The remains of a brisket of beef are excellent when cold.

No. 8. *Brisket of Beef à la Garrick.* This dish will, I am sure, be as popular with the English public as the celebrated tragedian and comedian whose name I have borrowed, even if he were now alive. Procure a nice brisket of beef with as little fat as possible attached, if too much cut a little of it off, and detach the whole of the bones from it, then make a pickle with twenty pounds of salt, three quarters of a pound of saltpetre, four cakes of sal prunella, two pounds of moist sugar, and two cloves of garlic, with which rub the meat well, and leave it rather more than a week, rubbing and turning it over every day; then drain and cut it into two equal parts, place one upon the other, mixing the fat and lean well, tie them together, and afterwards in a clean cloth, put into a large stewpan or stock-pot containing six gallons of water, and let simmer for eight hours, (but to ascertain correctly if done run a trussing-needle into it, if tender it is quite done;), then take it out and let it remain ten minutes upon a dish to drain, have ready a large tin dish-cover, eighteen inches long, twelve wide, and deep in proportion, place it upon a trivet and put the beef into it, opening the cloth to lie smoothly in the cover, and with a fork arranging the meat, fat and lean together, all over the bottom; you have a common piece of board half an inch in thickness made to fit into the cover, place it upon the meat with half a hundred weight upon it, and let remain in a cold place until the next morning, then take off the weight and the board, pull the cloth gently at each angle, and when loose turn it over upon your dish, take the cloth off gently, garnish with sprigs of parsley, fresh watercresses, and small radishes (if in season), cut in thin strips crosswise. Nothing could be nicer than this for a breakfast or luncheon, it will keep good a fortnight in winter, and as long as a week in the summer by putting it in a cold place. I have frequently made some in my Kitchen at Home, procuring a piece weighing ten or twelve pounds, from the bones and trimmings of which I have also made very excellent soup, which but of course must be fresh. The pickling will answer to salt three or four other joints, as it will keep good nearly a month in summer, and much longer in winter.

No. 9. *Haunch of Mutton.* The haunch is the most important joint from the sheep, it requires but little trimming, and to be hung about three weeks (season permitting). Saw about three inches from the knuckle, detach all the skin from the loin, and put it upon a spit, commencing running the spit in at the knuckle and bringing it out at the flap, avoiding the fillet of the loin (a cradle spit may be used for this joint,) set it down at the distance of two feet from a good solid fire, and if weighing about twenty pounds it requires two hours and a half roasting, ten minutes after it is down rub it over with butter, which you have fixed in the bowl of a wooden spoon, it will form a kind of froth over it, then place it back three feet from the fire, where let it continue until done, if approved of, shake over a little flour from a flour-dredge a quarter of an hour before taking it up, when done dress upon your dish with a paper frill upon the knuckle and about half a pint of gravy under. If the meat is rather fat the butter may be omitted.

No. 10. *Soyer's Saddle-back of Mutton.* This is an entirely new joint which I have introduced in this present month, April 1846. I have served it but three times in our coffee-room, where it gave the greatest satisfaction to those who had partaken of it, having dined from fifteen to eighteen each, whilst two saddles, which would weigh six or eight pounds more, would not dine more than seven or eight if badly carved, or more than ten if properly carved in the usual manner. The cut is a correct representation of the appearance of the new joint, which serves to indicate the mode of carving. It is composed of the two loins and two necks of a sheep trimmed into the form of a double saddle, without interfering in the least with the legs and shoulders, which would cause a serious loss to the butcher.

Trim and dispose the saddle-back as follows: saw the centre bone of the back as far as the saddle, dividing it but not cutting the meat or making a hole through, then with a small saw divide each joint, so as to admit of the necks being cut into chops in carving, when well separated take a piece of a good length from the ends of the rib bones, trim the flaps, turn them under, fixing them with skewers and string, giving the proper shape as the design represents, pull the skin from the whole back, melt two ounces of butter, which rub over with a paste brush to give a good appearance and let remain five or six days previous to roasting, weather permitting. To roast, pass a long saddle-of-mutton spit through the spinal-marrow-bone, bringing it out at the ends of the necks, fix it to a larger spit, and place at a good distance from a moderate fire for nearly three hours; avoid basting, but a quarter of an hour before taking up shake a little flour mixed with some finely-ground rice over, which is very good for a little change. This joint looks very noble, and does not appear too large when roasted. For a small dinner a saddleback of Welsh mutton or lamb will make a very fine remove. To carve, commence by passing your knife down the back where nothing but the meat and skin holds it together, and from thence crosswise to the flap, serving a cutlet and a slice between to each person, continuing the same way through the saddle; you will thus carve the meat according to the grain, and produce fresh hot gravy for each person as you proceed carving. Should any remain, it is fit either to be sent cold to table or dressed otherwise advantageously.

No. 11. *Saddle of Mutton.* Procure a fine saddle of mutton, about fourteen pounds in weight, that has been kept some time, take off the skin with a knife, and skewer the flaps under, run a lark-spit through the spinal marrow-bone, which spit affix to a larger one, and place down to roast as directed for the saddle-back; it will require about an hour and three quarters roasting, and must be carved as in the last.

No. 12. *Leg of Mutton.* A leg weighing eight pounds would take about an hour and a half roasting; run the spit in under the thigh-bone and bring it out at the knuckle, roast it as described for the haunch, and send to table with a frill upon the knuckle.

When I have a leg of mutton to roast in my kitchen I make a small incision at the knuckle two or three days before roasting, in which I put two or three cloves of garlic, it will give the mutton a fine and peculiar flavour, not at all resembling the strong, and to some objectionable, flavour of garlic. I frequently serve it with haricot beans under it, dressed as directed (No. 1094).

No. 13. *Shoulder of Mutton* of seven or eight pounds weight will require about one hour roasting; run the spit in at the flap and bring it out at the knuckle, observe the same directions as before, not basting, but merely rubbing it over with the butter.

No. 14. *Loin of Mutton.* A loin weighing six pounds would require an hour to roast; take off all the skin with a knife, and separate the joints with a chopper, not cutting through the fillet; run a lark-spit through from one extremity to the other and affix it to a larger spit, observe the same directions in roasting as for the haunch. This is a very favorite dish of mine at home, where I in general joint it with a meat-saw so as to enable me to carve it into thin slanting chops, which look so much more inviting in the plate than those huge pieces which are generally carved.

No. 15. *Neck of Mutton.* This I call a very recherché little joint when well kept; it must be nicely trimmed, sawing through the bones at the tips of the ribs, which detach from the meat, folding the flap over; saw off the chine-bone, and with a knife detach the remainder of the bone from the fillet, detach the skin from the upper part, fix the flap under with a couple of skewers, run a long flat iron skewer through the centre, from one extremity to the other, fix it to a larger spit, roast (if weighing five pounds) nearly three quarters of an hour, observing the same directions as before, carve it crosswise, cutting it in cotelettes, one of which, with a bone, serve to each guest.

No. 16. *Boiled Leg of Mutton.* Cut the knuckle from a leg of mutton which has been hung some time, put into an oval braising-pan well covered with cold water, in which you have put two ounces of salt, place it upon a sharp fire until boiling, when skim well, and place it upon the corner of the fire to simmer about two hours, that is, if the leg does not exceed more than nine pounds in weight; about half an hour before it is done add a dozen turnips, peeled and cut into quarters, when done take it up, dress upon a dish with the turnips around, place a frill upon the knuckle, pour nearly half a pint of the liquor it was boiled in over, and serve with caper sauce (No. 67) in a boat. Observe, in boiling any description of meat, fast boiling would not cook it any quicker, but cause it to eat very hard and bad.

At home I have tried to cook them by placing them in the water whilst boiling, and when again beginning to boil drawing it to the corner of the fire; it certainly saves a little time, but does not eat so tender as when put into cold water. I generally there mash turnips and serve them separately (I do not like them plain and watery, although I consider they must be much more wholesome). Place the turnips when boiled into a stewpan, add half a teaspoonful of salt, a quarter ditto of pepper, two ounces of butter with which you have mixed half a tablespoonful of flour, and four tablespoonfuls of cream or milk, mix all well together over the fire with a wooden spoon. For caper sauce I mix a tablespoonful of flour with an ounce of butter and put it in a smallish stewpan, add half a pint of the liquor the mutton was boiled in, stir over the fire until upon the point of boiling, when add a quarter of a tablespoonful of salt, quarter that quantity of pepper, a little grated nutmeg, and a good spoonful of drained pickled capers; then add another ounce of butter, shake round over the fire, and when melted it is finished. I sometimes also add a spoonful of liaison, it gives it a rich colour.

No. 17. *Shoulder of Mutton (boiled)*. Choose a very tender one, weighing about seven pounds, cut off the knuckle, and boil it as above; one hour and a half would be sufficient.

WELSH MUTTON.—No. 18. *Saddle-back of Welsh Mutton*. Trim and truss it as South Down mutton, it will take one hour less roasting; you may butter twice over.

No. 19. *Haunch*. If weighing twelve pounds roast it an hour and a half as directed (in proportion) for the haunch of mutton, but if deficient of fat rub it over with butter three or four times instead of once.

No. 20. *Saddle*. If weighing eight pounds roast it an hour and a quarter.

No. 21. *Leg*. If weighing five pounds roast it an hour.

No. 22. *Loin*. If weighing four pounds roast three quarters of an hour.

No. 23. *Neck*. If weighing three pounds roast it half an hour.

No. 24. *Shoulder*. If weighing four pounds roast it three quarters of an hour. Loin and neck about the same time.

No. 25. *Lamb* is divided into but three principal joints, being the forequarter, haunch, and saddle, two joints may be made of each by separating the shoulder from the ribs, the leg from the loin, or dividing the saddle, but they are usually roasted together.

To trim the fore-quarter saw off the chine-bone, and break the rib-bones down the centre, pass two iron skewers from the breast to the back, and a lark-spit through lengthwise, fix it upon a larger spit, cover a sheet of buttered paper over the top, and roast an hour and a quarter before a good fire, rubbing butter over it, it would be a light gold colour; should the shoulder have been taken off it will only require three quarters of an hour to roast, serve in a dish with a little gravy under, and mint sauce in a boat.

The haunch must be trimmed by cutting off the shank-bone, place it upon a small spit by running the spit in at the extremity of the loin, passing over the thigh-bone, and bringing it out at the knuckle, which tie to the spit with a piece of string; place a sheet of buttered paper over, and roast an hour and three-quarters before a solid fire; place a frill upon the knuckle, and serve as before. The leg only would require one hour roasting.

For the saddle, skewer the flaps underneath, curling each one round, run a lark-spit through the spinal marrow-bone, and fix it to a larger spit; place a sheet of buttered paper over, and roast an hour and a half before a good fire, dress upon your dish and serve as for the fore-quarter.

No. 26. *Fillet of Veal.* Choose it of the best quality, as described at the commencement of this series. Procure a leg, saw off the knuckle, take out the bone in the centre of the fillet, and fill up the cavity with some stuffing made as directed (No. 127), fold the udder and flap round, which fix with three skewers; place half a sheet of buttered foolscap paper top and bottom, which tie over and over with plenty of string, run a spit through, fixing the fillet with a hold-fast, set down to roast, placing it rather close to the fire ten minutes, rub well over with butter, then place it at least two feet and a half from the fire, to roast very slowly, giving it a fine gold colour; a fillet weighing sixteen pounds would require three hours roasting, when done, take it up, detach all the string and paper, trim the top and set it upon your dish; have a pint of melted butter in a stewpan upon the fire, to which, when boiling, add four spoonfuls of Harvey sauce, and two of mushroom catsup, mix well, and pour round the fillet; have also boiled nicely an ox-tongue, which skin and trim, dress upon a dish surrounded with greens or cabbage nicely boiled, and serve as an accompaniment to the fillet.

In my small kitchen I, however, content myself with a nice piece of streaked bacon, of about two pounds in weight, boiled and served surrounded with greens or turnip-tops if in season. For the different modes of dressing the remainder, see the Entrées, Kitchen at Home.

No. 27. *Loin of Veal.* Procure one with plenty of fat and a nice kidney in it, cut off the chump, take away the rib-bone at the other extremity, and fasten the flap over the kidney with a skewer, run a spit through lengthwise (not too thick a one), commencing at the thickest end, and fixing it at the other extremity with a hold-fast, tie it up in a sheet of oiled paper; if weighing fourteen pounds it will require two hours and a quarter to roast, serve with sauce and tongue, or bacon, as in the last, upon a separate dish. At home I usually content myself with the chump, as taken from the loin, either roasting or boiling it, should it weigh four pounds it would require an hour roasting, or an hour and a quarter boiling; if roasted, serve with bacon and the same sauce as for the fillet, but if boiled I make half the quantity of sauce as for boiled leg of mutton, but omitting the capers, and adding a spoonful of roughly-chopped, fresh, green parsley. Dress the remains the second day as directed in the Entrées, Kitchen at Home.

No. 28. *Breast of Veal.* Procure a nice breast of veal, which trim as directed (No. 455), stuff the interior with a long roll of stuffing (No. 127), roll the flaps over and sew it up with a trussing-needle and string, place it upon a spit, running it through lengthwise, and roast one hour and a quarter as directed for the loin, serve with the same sauce, and bacon and greens separate. The breast of veal stewed is also good, but for the details I must refer to the Removes in the first part of this work. At home I stew them, and add a few heads of celery with the stock it is stewing in, which I afterwards dress round the veal, and make a little white sauce similar to No. 7, with some of the liquor it was stewed in, or thicken the sauce with a little butter and flour, and add a gill of milk.

No. 29. *Shoulder of Veal.* A shoulder weighing fourteen pounds would require two hours and a half to roast, and three hours to boil, serve with a parsley and butter sauce if boiled, or if roasted, with sauce as for the fillet; bacon and greens must be served with it separate, whichever way it is dressed.

Should you boil the shoulder add a few vegetables, and you may reduce the stock it was boiled in to a glaze (by continual boiling), which will be very serviceable in dressing the remains upon following days; by boiling a calf's foot with the shoulder you would produce a much greater quantity of glaze.

No. 30. *Neck of Veal* is usually served as the shoulder, either roasted or stewed, with vegetables, but I have described a number of methods of dressing it in the Removes of the first department of this work.

No. 31. *Knuckle of Veal* is a very favorite dish of mine; I procure two of them, which I saw into three pieces each, and put into a stewpan with a piece of streaked bacon two pounds in weight, four onions, a carrot, two turnips, and six peppercorns, place over the fire, and when boiling add a little salt, skim well, and place at the corner to simmer gently for two hours, take up, dress them in your dish surrounded with the vegetables and bacon, and serve with parsley and butter over; very good soup may be made from the stock it was boiled in if required, or if not, into glaze, which put by until wanted.

No. 32. *Leg of Pork.* Choose the pork as described at the commencement of this series, if a leg, one weighing about seven pounds, cut an incision in the knuckle near the thigh, into which put a quantity of sage and onions, previously passed in butter, sew the incision up with packthread, score the rind of the pork in lines across, half an inch apart, place upon a spit, running it in just under the rind, and bringing it out at the knuckle. If stuffed the day previous to roasting it would improve its flavour; roast, if weighing seven pounds, about two hours and a half, and serve with apple sauce in a boat.

I often roast a small leg of pork at home as directed above, and make apple sauce thus: peel and slice six nice apples, which put into a stewpan, with a tablespoonful of currants well washed and picked, and one of brown sugar, a little of the rind of a lemon chopped very fine, six spoonfuls of water, and a very small piece of cinnamon, boil until in purée, then stir in a handful of bread-crumbs, and serve hot. When, however, I am in a great hurry I merely put apples, water, sugar, and a little rind of lemon. Other joints of pork are roasted in the same manner, but do not require stuffing, a loin weighing six pounds requiring two hours and a quarter to roast; a neck of the same size will take about the same time, as will the spare-ribs, which is nothing but the necks of larger pork with the blade-bone cut out and the fat taken off.

No. 33. *Salt Pork.* Pork is salted in the same manner as described for beef, omitting the saltpetre, but of course not requiring so long a time; a leg weighing seven pounds would be well salted in a week, as also would a hand and spring weighing about ten pounds, and either would require two hours boiling, putting them in a stewpan with cold water, and serving with carrots and greens upon a separate dish. With the leg it is also customary to serve a pease pudding made thus: tie about a pint of split peas loosely in a pudding-cloth, throw them into boiling water to stew until tender, then take them up, turn from the cloth upon the back of a hair sieve, through which force them with a wooden spoon, put them into a basin, add two ounces of butter, season with pepper and salt, mix well with six whole eggs, tie up tightly in a pudding-cloth, boil an hour and serve very hot.

A pig's head is also excellent pickled. Divide the head in two, take out the brains and detach the jaw-bones, pickle it twelve days, rubbing it every day, (the brine in which you have pickled one joint, with the addition of more salt, would pickle several and keep good for upwards of a month;) when ready, boil it nearly three hours, and serve with greens round as an accompaniment to veal or poultry. To pickle it red, rub it well with twelve pounds of salt, a quarter of a pound of saltpetre, two cakes of sal prunella, and half a pound of coarse sugar, rub it every day, allowing it to remain fifteen days in pickle, after which it maybe hung, and dried or smoked previously to dressing.

MADE DISHES THAT CAN BE EASILY PREPARED AT A MODERATE EXPENSE IN MY KITCHEN AT HOME.

Preaching economy which has been practised from age to age in all domestic works is not here my intention, as my readers must quickly perceive that the simplicity of my receipts excludes the seal of extravagance, having simplified even dishes of some importance, which daily give and have given the greatest satisfaction at the Reform Club.

The regular courses of a cuisine bourgeoise, or domestic cookery, will be found extremely easy to execute in my Kitchen at Home, and numbers of them done to perfection in the Kitchen (or sanctorum) of a Bachelor, as well as in the small Cottage Kitchen.

No. 34. *French Pot-au-feu.* Out of this earthen pot comes the favorite soup and bouilli, which have been everlastingly famed as having been the support of several generations of all classes of society in France; from the opulent to the poorest individuals, all pay tribute to its excellence and worth. In fact this soup and bouilli are to the French what the roast beef and plum-pudding are on a Sunday to the English. No dinner in France is served without soup, and no good soup is supposed to be made without the pot-au-feu. Generally every quarter of a century makes a total alteration in fashions and politics, need I say also in cookery, which must be approximated not only to the fashion but more strongly so to the political world, humbly bending its indispensable services to the whims and wishes of crowned heads, which invariably lead the multitude; for example, the bills of fare of the sumptuous dinners which used to grace the tables of Louis the Fourteenth, Sixteenth, and Eighteenth, of France, were all very different to each other, and none of them were ever copied to grace the sumptuous and luxurious tables of the Empire; even the very features of them having undergone an entire change in our own days; every culinary invention taking its title and origin from some celebrated personage or extraordinary event, every innovation in cookery, like a change in fashion, causing us to forget those dishes which they have superseded; I have no doubt but that, if some correct historian could collect the bills of fare of dinners from various centuries and nations which crowned heads have partaken of, he might write a very interesting volume under the title of History of Cookery, in which we should be able closely to trace the original history of different countries.[23] Nothing can stamp the anniversary of any great event so well as a sumptuous banquet: peace, war, politics, and even religion, have always been the cause of extraordinary and sometimes monstrous gastronomic meetings; for a proof of which my readers will find at the end of this work a correct bill of fare (found in the Tower of London,) of a dinner given by the Earl of Warwick at the installation of an Archbishop of York, in the year 1470. In time of war artists are engaged sketching on immense canvasses the horrors and disasters of a battle, while in peace they sketch the anniversary banquets for the victorious, in honour of the event, (reminding us of the calm after a storm;) and we may sincerely hope, for the credit of humanity at large, that a disastrous battle may have its hundreds of anniversary banquets without a fresh combat. But to return to the humble but indispensable science of cookery. Everything seems to prove to us that it has always performed an important part in political events, and has been exposed to as many alterations; still, amongst so many changes, it is with a national pleasure that I find, amongst the heap of frivolous culinary ruins, an old favorite of our great great-grandfathers still remaining ours, having boldly passed through every storm, it has for ever established its culinary power upon our changeable soil. The brown cheek of this demi-immortal is daily seen ornamenting the firesides of millions, and merely acquaints the children the first thing in the morning that something good is in preparation for their dinner: this mighty vessel is called in French *pot-au-feu*,[24] in which is made that excellent and wholesome luxury which for centuries has been the principal nourishment and support of the middling and poorer classes of France at a very trifling expense. It is not upon the tables of the wealthy that the best of this national soup is to be obtained, but upon the right or left side of the entrance to his noble mansion, in a square, oval, or octagonal room, commonly called *la Loge du Portier*, or the Porter's Lodge; as nearly every porter has his portière, that is, a wife who answers the door (whilst her husband is doing the frottage, or polishing the floor of the apartment), while pulling the string or wire which loosens the lock to let people in with one hand, she skims the *pot-au-feu* with the other; should she be fortunate enough to possess two eyes she would keep one upon her *pot-*

au-feu, and the other upon the individual, who had, probably, come only to make inquiry; but unfortunately for La Mère Binard (whom I shall have the pleasure of introducing to my readers as a gastronomic wonder in her simple style), she had but one eye, which she almost entirely devoted to the ebullition of her *pot-au-feu*; having been portière there two-and-thirty years, she knew most of the people in the habit of calling by their voice, and used to answer them even without turning her shaking head. But what brought her domestic cookery in such high repute, that she was not to be excelled by any portière of Paris, was, that one day her master, M. le Comte de C**** (who was a good gentleman and great epicure), came home from a long ride while she was performing her humble occupation of pouring the soup into the tureen; a triple knock came to the door, which immediately opened as by electricity, and in walked her beloved master, who came to the door of the lodge to pay his duties to his old and faithful servant, whilst an exhalation of the most delicious fragrance perfumed the small apartment from the boiling consommé which attracted his scientific attention; after a short inquiry he discovered in an old brown pan the gloriously smoking hot consommé, and seizing with avidity a spoon by the side, tasted (much to the astonishment of La Mère Binard) several spoonfuls, pronouncing the first delicious, the second excellent, the third delightful, in fact, magnificent. "Can you spare any of it?" he said, addressing the worthy dame. "Yes," said she, "but I am sure Monseigneur does not mean it." "But indeed I do," replied he; "and if I had been aware I could have obtained such a treasure, I would have had nothing else for my dinner to-day; and if you were not so far advanced in years I would not object to make you a *cordon bleu*." The earthen pan was immediately conveyed up stairs to the dining-room, and deposited upon the table of his seigneurie, where an excellent dinner was waiting for himself and friends; but the immortal *pot-au-feu*, resting on a superb silver tray, with its handle half broken off, made all the homage of the dinner, to the great annoyance of the cook, who had thus sacrificed the art he had displayed in dressing a most recherché dinner, and felt much offended at the whim of his wealthy master, who had neglected his dinner to take pot-luck with his porter's wife.

By a friendly introduction to La Mère Binard, I, with a great deal of supplication, obtained from her the following valuable receipt, having been obliged first to listen to the constant repetition of the above anecdote before she could explain it to me.—"I generally choose," says she, "a bit of the *gite à la noix,* part of the aitch-bone, a piece of the rump, or a slice from the thickest part of the leg, weighing from four to five pounds, with sufficient fat attached, or adding a small piece; then I put it into the earthen pan, and fill with cold water till within two inches of the rim, being about four quarts; then I set it by my wood fire until beginning to get hot, when a thin scum will arise by degrees, which I carefully take off and throw away; then I add half a pound of beef liver, and a tablespoonful and a half of salt, it will produce more scum, which also carefully remove; have ready prepared, well washed and clean, two middling-sized carrots cut in halves, then in four, two small pieces of parsnip, four turnips, two onions, with two cloves stuck in each, eight young leeks, or two old ones, a head of celery cut into pieces three inches in length, tie the leeks and celery into a bunch, and put altogether into the *pot-au-feu,* set it alone nearer the fire until it commences boiling, skim again, draw it a little farther to the corner of the fire, put a wooden skimmer across the pot, upon which rest the lid to prevent its boiling fast, (which would entirely spoil the soup, the meat becoming very hard and the soup thick and muddy)." "You quite astonish me, Mrs. Binard," said I. "Oh," says she, "I have had so many years of experience, and I know it to be the case." "Yes," said I, "my dear lady, I do not in the least doubt your correctness." "Well, then, one hour afterwards I add a little cold water to keep it to the same quantity, put in a burnt onion to give it a colour, and let simmer four hours, sometimes five, depending if the meat is cut very thick; then I cut some large thin slices of bread, which I lay at the bottom of the tureen, then I take off the greater part of the fat, cut the bunch of celery and leeks open, lay them upon the slices of bread, with one of the carrots, two turnips, and the pieces of parsnip; take half of the broth with a ladle, which pour into the tureen, (there being quite enough soup for six of us, myself, Binard, my daughter and her husband, and the two boys); then I take out carefully the meat, which I lay upon the dish, with half of the liver at the side, the other half, when cold, I give to Minette (her favorite cat), lay the remainder of the vegetables round, with some fine sprigs of fresh parsley; by that time the bread is (trempé) moistened; set both upon the table at once, keeping the meat covered until we have done with the soup: that is the way we dine upon a Sunday. The next day, with the remainder of the broth I make vermicelli or rice soup, or the same with bread in it, and fricassée the remainder of the beef in various ways. When my daughter was ill I used to put a calf's foot in the *pot-au-feu* with the beef; it made the soup very strengthening and did her much good." "Will you be kind enough," said I, "to tell me where you get these burnt onions, for I perceive without it your soup would be quite white." "Bless you, sir!" she replied, "you may get six for two sous at any of the grocers, or you can burn them yourself in the oven, or by the fireside, gently turning them now and then until they are quite black, but not burnt to a cinder, or it would spoil the flavour of the soup." I then took leave of her, returning thanks for her kindness, and put down the receipt as she gave it me during her long explanation, as follows:

RECEIPT. Put in the *pot-au-feu* six pounds of beef, four quarts of water, set near the fire; skim, when nearly boiling add a spoonful and a half of salt, half a pound of liver, two carrots, four turnips, eight young or two old leeks, one head of celery, two onions and one burnt, with a clove in each, and a piece of parsnip; skim again and let simmer four or five hours, adding a little cold water now and then; take off part of the fat, put slices of bread into the tureen, lay half the vegetables over, and half the broth, and serve the meat separate with the vegetables around. Since I have been in England I have broken my precious earthen pot; I have, however, made some very good soups at home in a black saucepan or stewpan, but must admit not quite so delicate and perfect as in the identical *pot de terre*.

SOUPS.—No. 35. *Julienne Soup.* Put about six pounds of knuckle of veal in a stewpan cut in four pieces, with about half a pound of streaked bacon; put a piece of butter at the bottom of the stewpan, and about half a pint of water, place it over a sharp fire, moving it round occasionally with a wooden spoon until the bottom of the stewpan is covered with a white glaze, when add about a gallon of water, two ounces of salt, three onions (with two cloves in each), two turnips, one carrot, a head of celery, leek, and a bunch of parsley, thyme, and bay-leaf; when boiling put in two burnt onions (see *Pot-au-feu*) to colour it, and stand it at the corner of the fire to simmer for two hours, keeping it well skimmed, then pass the broth through a hair sieve into a stewpan; you have previously cut two middling-sized carrots, two turnips, an onion, a leek, and a little celery into very thin strips an inch long; put them in another stewpan with two ounces of butter and a teaspoonful of powdered sugar; place it upon a sharp fire, tossing them over occasionally until well fried and looking transparent, then put them into the broth with the half a young cos lettuce, and a little tarragon and chervil, place it at the corner of your fire, and when it boils skim off all the butter:

let it simmer until the vegetables are perfectly tender, when pour it into your tureen; serve the veal and piece of bacon upon the dish with melted butter and chopped parsley over. Beef may also be used for the above, and the vegetables cut in any of the shapes directed for the soups in the other department of this work; if you only require a smaller quantity, take only three pounds, or diminish all in proportion.

No. 36. *Mutton Broth.* Any description of trimmings of mutton may be used for broth, but the scrag end of the neck is usually chosen. Put about two scrags into a stewpan (having previously jointed the bone), with three onions (a couple of cloves stuck in each), three turnips, one carrot, and a bunch containing a leek, a head of celery, and a few sprigs of thyme and parsley, fill up the stewpan with rather more than a gallon of water; when boiling skim it, and place it at the corner of the stove, where let it simmer for three hours, then cut a small carrot, two turnips, an onion, and a piece of leek and celery into very small square pieces, put them into a stewpan with a wineglassful of pearl barley, pass the broth through a hair sieve over them, and boil at the corner of the fire until the barley is tender, when it is ready to serve; the meat may be trimmed into neat pieces, and served in the broth, or separately with melted butter and parsley, or onion sauce.

No. 37. *Irish Mutton Broth.* This broth is made similar to the last, adding ten or twelve mealy potatoes cut in large dice, which by boiling to a purée thickens the broth; just before serving throw in twenty heads of parsley, at the same time put in a few flowers of marigolds, which really give a pleasing flavour; it is then ready to serve.

At home I make clear soup of the trimmings of any meat, either beef, veal, mutton, or lamb, or the trimmings of two or three different sorts of meat, in the same manner as directed for Julienne soup.

No. 38. *A very simple Receipt for the Scotch Cock-a-Leeky.* This is a very favorite national soup with the Scotch, which by rights ought to have been the pride of Welsh cookery, ranking as high in the estimation of millions as their celebrated and generally appreciated rarebit, commonly called a Welsh rabbit.

Take six or eight pounds of leg of beef (depending upon the quantity you want to make), with which make a stock as directed for Julienne soup, letting simmer two hours, and keeping it well skimmed; in the mean time trim two or three bunches of fine winter leeks, cutting off the roots and part of the head, then split each in halves lengthwise, and each half in three, wash well in two or three waters, pass the stock through a sieve into another stewpan, into which put the leeks, with a fowl trussed as for boiling, let simmer very gently at the corner of the fire for three hours, keeping it well skimmed, season a little if required, and half an hour before serving add two dozen French plums, without breaking them; when ready to serve, take out the fowl, which cut into neat pieces, place in a large tureen, and pour the leeks and broth over, the leeks being then partly in purée; if too thick, however, add a drop more broth or water. Should the leeks happen to be old and strong, it would be better to blanch them five minutes in a gallon of boiling water previously to putting them with the stock. Although an old cock is usually procured in Scotland for the above purpose, I prefer a young one, but should an old one be most handy, stew it a short time in the stock before passing it.

No. 39. *Ox-tail Soup.* Cut up two ox-tails, separating them at the joint, put a small piece of butter at the bottom of a stewpan, then put in the ox-tails, with a carrot, turnip, three onions, head of celery, one leek, and a bunch of parsley, thyme, and bay-leaf, add half a pint of water and twelve grains of whole pepper, set over a sharp fire, stirring occasionally until the bottom of the stewpan is covered with a thickish brown glaze; then add a quarter of a pound of flour, stir it well in, and fill up the stewpan with three quarts of water, add a tablespoonful of salt, stir occasionally until boiling, when set it upon the corner of the stove, skim well, and let simmer until the tails are stewed very tender, the flesh coming easily from the bone; take them out immediately and put them into your tureen; pass the soup, which must not be too thick, through a hair sieve over them, add a head of celery previously cut small and blanched in a little stock, and serve.

Ox-tail soup may also be made clear by omitting the flour, and serving vegetables in it as directed in Julienne soup (No. 35), but cut in any other shape.

No. 40. *Ox-cheek Soup.* Blanch and wash well two ox-cheeks, cut off the beard, take away all the bone, which chop up, and cut the flesh into middling-sized pieces, leaving the cheek part whole, put altogether into a stewpan, with four quarts of water, a little salt, ten peppercorns, two carrots, two turnips, one leek, one head of celery, and a bunch of parsley, thyme, and bay-leaf, also a burnt onion to colour it; let stew at the corner of the fire six hours, keeping well skimmed, then take out the fleshy part of the cheek and pass the broth through a hair sieve into another stewpan, mix half a pound of flour with a pint of cold broth, which pour into it and stir over the fire until boiling, place it at the corner, let simmer till tender (adding two heads of celery cut very fine, and a glass of sherry); when the celery is tender, cut the meat in small square slices, keep them warm, and when the soup is ready pour over and serve. Sheep's or lambs' heads also make very good soup by following the above receipt, and adding two pounds of veal, mutton, or beef to the stock, two heads would be sufficient, and they would not require so long to stew.

No. 41. *New Mock Turtle Soup.* Procure half a calf's head (scalded, not skinned), bone it, then cut up a knuckle of veal, which put into a stewpan, with half a pound of lean ham, two ounces of butter, one of salt, at the bottom, a carrot, one turnip, three onions, a head of celery, a leek, and a bunch of parsley, thyme, marjoram, basil, and a bay-leaf, with nearly half a pint of water; move round occasionally upon the fire until the bottom of the stewpan is covered with a white glaze; then add six quarts of water, and put in the half head, let simmer at the corner of the fire for two hours and a half, or till the head is perfectly tender, when take it up and press it between two dishes, pass the stock through a hair sieve into a basin; then in another stewpan have a quarter of a pound of butter, with a sprig of thyme, basil, marjoram, and a bay-leaf, let the butter get quite hot; then add six ounces of flour to form a roux, stir over a sharp fire a few minutes, keeping it quite white, stand it off the fire to cool, then add the stock, boil up, skim, and pass it through a hair sieve into another stewpan, cut the head into pieces an inch square, not too thick, and put them into the soup, which season with a little cayenne pepper; when the pieces are hot, add a gill of cream, and pour it into your tureen. The above quantity will make several tureens of soup, and will keep good several days.

No. 42. *Brown Mock Turtle Soup.* Proceed the same as in the last article, only colouring the stock by drawing it down to a brown glaze, or with a couple of burnt onions, and serving with a glass of port wine in it, or two of sherry, omitting the cream.

No. 43. *Mulligatawny Soup.* Cut up a knuckle of veal, which put in a stewpan with a piece of butter, half a pound of lean ham, a carrot, one turnip, three onions, six apples, one head of celery, one leek, a bunch of parsley, thyme, and bay-leaf, a blade of mace, six cloves, and half a pint of water; set the stewpan over a sharp fire, move the meat round occasionally, let remain until the bottom of the stewpan is covered with a brownish glaze; then add two or three tablespoonfuls of currie powder, one of currie paste, if handy, and half a pound of flour, stir well in, and fill up with a gallon of water, add a spoonful of salt, half ditto of sugar, and a quarter ditto of pepper, let boil up; then place it at the corner of the stove, where let it simmer two hours and a half, then pass it through a hair sieve into the tureen; trim some of the pieces of veal, which serve in it, and some plain boiled rice separate; ox-tails or pieces of rabbits, chickens, &c., left from a previous dinner may be served in it instead of the veal; if too thick add a drop of broth or water.

No. 44. *Giblet Soup.* Clean two sets of giblets and soak for two hours, cut them into equal sizes and put them into a stewpan, with a quarter of a pound of butter, four pounds of veal or beef, half a pound of ham, a carrot, turnip, three onions, a head of celery, leek, two ounces of salt, and a bunch of parsley, thyme, and bay-leaf; place the stewpan over a sharp fire, stirring the meat round occasionally, when the bottom of the stewpan is covered with a light glaze add half a pound of flour, stir well in, and fill up with a gallon of water, add two burnt onions to colour it; when boiling set at the corner of the stove, let simmer, skim well, and when the giblets are tender take them out, put them in your tureen, pass the soup through a hair sieve over, and serve; twenty button onions, or any small sharp vegetable, is very good in it, also a glass of port wine.

No. 45. *Green Pea Soup.* Put two quarts of green peas into a stewpan with a quarter of a pound of butter, quarter of a pound of lean ham cut in dice, two onions in slices, and a few sprigs of parsley; add a quart of cold water, and with the hand rub all well together, then pour off the water, cover the stewpan close and stand it upon a sharp fire, tossing or stirring them round occasionally; when very tender add two or three tablespoonfuls of flour, mix well in, mashing the peas with your spoon against the sides of the stewpan, add three quarts of broth, made as for Julienne soup (No. 35), or broth from the pot-au-feu (No. 34), and a tablespoonful of sugar, with a little pepper and salt if required, boil all well together five minutes; then rub it through a tammie or hair sieve, put it into another stewpan with half a pint of boiling milk, boil and skim, then pour it into your tureen, and serve with small croutons of fried bread-crumbs. It must not be served too thick.

No. 46. *Winter Pea Soup.* Wash a quart of split peas, which put into a stewpan with half a pound of streaked bacon, two onions in slices, two pounds of veal or beef cut into small pieces, and a little parsley, thyme, and bay-leaf, previously passed in butter in the same stewpan; cover with a gallon of water, add a little salt and sugar, place it upon the fire; when boiling stand it at the side until the peas are boiled to a purée, and the water has reduced to half, then take out the meat, place it in the tureen, keep it hot, and rub the soup through a hair sieve or tammie, put it into another stewpan, and when boiling pour over the meat and serve. The bacon is good cold, the meat may also be put into the tureen if approved of.

No. 47. *Purée, or Vegetable Soup.* Peel and cut up very fine three onions, three turnips, one carrot, and four potatoes, put them into a stewpan with a quarter of a pound of butter, the same of lean ham, and a bunch of parsley, pass them ten minutes over a sharp fire; then add a good spoonful of flour, mix well in, moisten with two quarts of broth (prepared as for Julienne soup, No. 35), and a pint of boiling milk, boil up, keeping it stirred, season with a little salt and sugar, and rub through a hair sieve or tammie, put it into another stewpan, boil again, skim, and serve with croutons of fried bread in it.

No. 48. *Soup Maigre.* Cut two onions into very small dice and put them into a stewpan with two ounces of butter, fry them a short time, but not to change colour; have three or four handfuls of well-washed sorrel, cut it into ribands, and put it into the stewpan with the onions, add two tablespoonfuls of flour, mix well, then a pint of milk and a pint of water, boil all together ten minutes, season with a little sugar and salt, and finish with a liaison of two yolks of eggs, mixed with a gill of cream, stir it in quickly, do not let it boil afterwards; put the crust of a French roll cut in strips into your tureen, pour the soup over, and serve.

No. 49. *Onion Soup Maigre.* Peel and cut ten large onions into small dice, put them into a stewpan with a quarter of a pound of butter, place them over the fire, fry them well; then add three tablespoonfuls of flour, which mix well, and rather better than a quart of water, boil till the onions are quite tender, season with a little salt and sugar, finish with a liaison, and serve as in the last; grated cheese is an improvement in it.

No. 50. *Vermicelli Soup.* Make your stock as for Julienne soup (No. 35), when passed put it into another stewpan with two ounces of vermicelli, boil it a quarter of an hour, then pour it into your tureen, and serve.

Semolina or tapioca soup is made the same, using either instead of vermicelli. For rice soup, see No. 197, Kitchen of the Wealthy.

No. 51. *Macaroni Soup.* (See No. 198, and Italian Paste, No. 194, Kitchen of the Wealthy.)

FISH.—No. 52. *Turbot.* For the methods of cleaning fish, see the other department of this work. In My Kitchen at Home I should never think of cooking too large a turbot, but choose a middle-sized one which, generally speaking, is the best; cut an incision in the back, rub it well with a good handful of salt, then with the juice of a lemon, set it in a turbot kettle well covered with cold water, in which you have put a good handful of salt, place over the fire, and as soon as the water boils put it at the side; if a turbot of ten pounds it will take an hour after it has boiled, if it should be allowed to more than simmer it will be very unsightly; take out of the water, leave a minute upon your drainer, serve upon a napkin garnished with fresh parsley, and lobster sauce in a boat; for sauce (see No. 68), or shrimp sauce (No. 73).

No. 53. *Turbot, the new French Fashion.* Boil your turbot as in the last but dress it upon a dish without a napkin, sauce over with a thickish melted butter (having placed a border of well-boiled small potatoes round), sprinkle a few capers over and serve.

No. 54. *Turbot à la Crême* is done with the remains of a turbot from a previous dinner; detach the flesh from the bone, and warm in salt and water, make cream sauce as page 99, only omit a third of the butter.

Brills are cooked in the same manner as turbots, but being smaller do not require so long boiling; but in boiling any description of fish, never take it up until it leaves the bone with facility, which try by placing the point of a knife between the flesh and the bone, if done the flesh will detach immediately.

No. 55. *John Dorée, Boulogne fashion.* John Dorées, though not very handsome, are very delicate eating; choose them from four to six pounds in weight, and boil as directed for turbot; one of the above size would require about three quarters of an hour; if any remain, dress like turbot, or with caper sauce, &c.

No. 56. *Salmon, plain boiled.* I prefer always dressing this fish in slices from an inch or two inches in thickness, boiling it in plenty of salt and water about half an hour; the whole fish may be boiled, or the head and shoulders of a large fish, but they require longer boiling. Salmon eats firmer, by not being put into the water until boiling; dress the fish upon a napkin and serve with lobster sauce (page 30), shrimp do., or plain melted butter in a boat, with fresh sprigs of parsley boiled a few minutes in it. A salmon weighing ten pounds will require an hour and a half boiling; a head and shoulders weighing six pounds, one hour. The remains may be dressed à la crême, as directed for the turbot (No. 54).

No. 57. *Salmon Sauce Matelote.* Cook three good slices of salmon as directed in the last, or a large salmon peal trussed in the form of the letter S; dress it upon a dish without a napkin, having previously drained off all the water; have ready the following sauce: peel fifty small button onions, then put a good teaspoonful of powdered sugar into a convenient-sized stewpan, place it upon a sharp fire, and just as the sugar melts and turns yellowish add a quarter of a pound of butter and the onions, place it again upon the fire, tossing them over occasionally until they become slightly browned, then add a good tablespoonful of flour (mix well, but gently), a glass of sherry, and a pint of broth (reserved from some soup), let boil at the corner of the stove, skim well, and when the onions are done and the sauce rather thick, add a little pepper, salt, a teaspoonful of catsup, one of Harvey sauce, and one of essence of anchovies; when ready to serve add two dozen of oysters, blanched and bearded, allow them to get quite hot, sauce over and serve. I sometimes at home make a few fish quenelles (No. 124, Kitchen of the Wealthy) and add to the sauce.

The remainder of the above is very good if put in the oven upon a dish with a cover over and a little additional sauce.

No. 58. *Cod Fish, plain boiled.* (See page 119.)

No. 59. *Cod Fish sauced over with Oyster Sauce.* Boil three slices of the fish as above, drain and dress them upon a dish without a napkin, blanch three dozen oysters by putting them into a stewpan with their juice upon the fire, move them round occasionally, do not let them boil; as soon as they become a little firm place a sieve over a basin, pour in the oysters, beard and throw them again into their liquor, put them into a stewpan; when boiling add four cloves, half a blade of mace, six peppercorns, and two ounces of butter, to which you have added half a tablespoonful of flour, breaking it into small pieces, stir well together, when boiling, season with a little salt, cayenne pepper, and essence of anchovies, finish with a gill of cream, or milk, and sauce over. The remains of this fish may be taken from the bone and placed upon a dish, with a little of the above sauce (to which you have added the yolks of two eggs) over, sprinkle over with bread-crumbs, and place it twenty minutes in a hot oven till the bread-crumbs become brown.

For Salt Fish, see page 122, in the other department of this work.

No. 60. *Haddocks.* (See Nos. 308, 309, 310, Kitchen of the Wealthy.)

No. 61. *Baked Haddocks.* (See page 129.)

No. 62. *Soles, Fried.* (See page 114.)

No. 63. *Soles, the Jewish Fashion.* Trim the fish well, dip it into a couple of eggs, well beaten, put six tablespoonfuls of salad-oil in a sauté-pan, place it over the fire, and when quite hot put in your sole; let remain five minutes, turn over, and fry upon the other side; ten or twelve minutes will cook it according to the size; serve upon a napkin without sauce. They are excellent cold.

No. 64. *Sole à la Meunière.* (See page 115, in the other department of this work.)

No. 65. *Sole aux Fines Herbes*. Put a spoonful of chopped eschalots into a sauté-pan, with a glass of sherry and an ounce of butter, place the sole over, pour nearly half a pint of melted butter over it, upon which sprinkle some chopped parsley, place it in a moderate oven for half an hour, take the sole out of the pan, dress upon a dish without a napkin, reduce the sauce that is in the pan over a sharp fire, add a little Harvey sauce and essence of anchovy, pour over the sole, and serve them with a little flour and butter.

No. 66. *Fried Whiting*. The whiting requires to be skinned, and the tail turned round and fixed into the mouth, dip it first into flour, then egg over, and dip it into bread-crumbs, fry as directed for the sole; for whiting aux fines herbes proceed as directed for sole aux fines herbes. At home I prefer the whiting fried with their skins on, merely dipping them in flour.

No. 67. *Whiting au Gratin*. Put a good spoonful of chopped onions upon a strong earthen dish, with a glass of wine, season the whitings with a little pepper and salt, put it in the dish, sprinkle some chopped parsley and chopped mushrooms over, and pour over half a pint of anchovy sauce (page 32), over which sprinkle some brown bread-crumbs, grated from the crust of bread, place it in a warm oven half an hour; it requires to be nicely browned; serve upon the dish you have cooked it in.

No. 68. *Red Mullets*. Procure two red mullets, which place upon a strong dish not too large, sprinkle some chopped onions, parsley, a little pepper and salt, and a little salad-oil over, and put them into a warm oven for half an hour, then put a tablespoonful of chopped onions into a stewpan, with a teaspoonful of salad-oil, stir over a moderate fire until getting rather yellowish, then add a tablespoonful of sherry, half a pint of melted butter, with a little chopped mushrooms and parsley; reduce quickly over a sharp fire, keeping it stirred until becoming rather thick; when the mullets are done sauce over and serve.

No. 69. *Mackerel* are generally served plain boiled; put them in a kettle containing boiling water, well salted, let simmer nearly half an hour, take them up, drain, and dish them upon a napkin, serve melted butter in a boat, with which you have mixed a tablespoonful of chopped fennel, boiling it a few minutes.

No. 70. *Mackerel à la Maître d'Hôtel*. (See p. 127); as also for Mackerel au beurre noir.

No. 71. *Gurnets* are best stuffed and baked; stuff them as directed for haddocks, turn them round in the same manner, lay slices of butter over, cut very thin, and bake half an hour or more (according to their size) in a warm oven, when done dress upon a dish without a napkin, and have ready the following sauce: put a tablespoonful of chopped onions in a stewpan, with one of vinegar, place over the fire a couple of minutes, add half a pint of melted butter, a tablespoonful of Harvey sauce, one of catsup, and two of water, reduce until rather thick, season with a little pepper, cut the fillets of a good anchovy into strips, put in the sauce, which pour round the fish and serve.

No. 72. *Boiled Gurnet.* You may boil it either with or without the stuffing in very salt water, it will require rather more than half an hour; serve with anchovy sauce separate.

No. 73. *Herrings boiled with Cream Sauce.* Boil six herrings about twenty minutes in plenty of salt and water, but only just to simmer; then have ready the following sauce: put half a gill of cream upon the fire in a stewpan, when it boils add eight spoonfuls of melted butter, an ounce of fresh butter, a little pepper, salt, and the juice of half a lemon; dress the fish upon a dish without a napkin, sauce over and serve.

For Broiled Herrings à la Digon, see page 132.

No. 74. *Skate* is usually crimped, cut into long slices, and curled round; procure two or three slices, tie them with string to keep the shape in boiling, put them into a kettle of boiling water, in which you have put a good handful of salt; boil gently about twenty minutes (have ready also a piece of the liver, which boil with it), when done drain well, and put it upon a dish without a napkin; put three parts of a pint of melted butter in a stewpan, place it upon the fire, and when quite hot add a wineglassful of capers, sauce over and serve.

For Skate au beurre noir, see page 133.

Skate may also be served upon a napkin with a boat of well-seasoned melted butter, to which you have added a spoonful of Harvey sauce.

No. 75. *Flounders, Water Souchet.* Procure four or six Thames flounders, cut each in halves, put half a pint of water in a sauté-pan, with a little scraped horseradish, a little pepper, salt, sugar, and forty sprigs of fresh parsley; place over the fire, boil a minute, then add the flounders, stew ten minutes, take them out and place in a dish without a napkin, reduce the liquor they were stewed in a little, pour over and serve.

To fry flounders, trim them, and proceed precisely as directed for fried soles (p. 114).

Smelts are likewise floured, egged, bread-crumbed, and fried as above.

Plaice are plain boiled in salt and water, and served with shrimp sauce in a boat.

FRESH WATER FISH.—No. 76. *Pike.* Clean as directed (page 93), stuff the interior as directed for haddocks (page 129), only adding some fillets of anchovies and chopped lemon-peel with it; curl round and put in a baking dish, spread a little butter all over, put in a moderate oven; when about half done egg over with a paste brush, and sprinkle bread-crumbs upon it; a middling-sized pike will take about an hour, but that according to the size and the heat of the oven; when done dress upon a dish without a napkin, and sauce round as directed for baked haddock above referred to.

No. 77. *Pike, Sauce Matelote.* Cook a pike exactly as in the last, dress it upon a dish without a napkin, and sauce with a matelote sauce over, made as directed for salmon sauce matelote (No. 57).

This fish may also be served with caper sauce as directed for the skate (No. 74)—the smaller ones are the best; the remains of a pike placed in the oven the next day, with a cover over it and a little more sauce added, is very nice.

No. 78. *Stewed Carp.* Procure a good-sized carp, stuff it, then put it into a baking-dish with two onions, one carrot, one turnip, one head of celery, and a good bunch of parsley, thyme, and bay-leaf; moisten with two glasses of port wine, and put it in a moderate oven about two hours to bake; try if done with a knife, which is the case if the flesh leaves the bone easily, dress upon a dish without a napkin, then have ready the following sauce: mince a large Spanish onion with two common ones, and put them into a stewpan with three spoonfuls of salad-oil, fry rather a yellow colour, add two glasses of port wine and two spoonfuls of flour, mix all well together, add a pint of broth (reserved from some soup) or water, with half an ounce of glaze, boil it up, drain the stock the carp was cooked in from the vegetables, which also add to the sauce; boil well at the corner of the stove, skim, and when rather thick add a teaspoonful of Harvey sauce, one of essence of anchovies, twelve pickled mushrooms, and a little cayenne pepper, pour all the liquor drained from the fish out of your dish, sauce over and serve.

No. 79. *Carp, Sauce Matelote.* Put your carp into a small oval fish-kettle, with wine and vegetables as in the last, to which add also a pint of water and a little salt, with a few cloves and peppercorns; put the lid upon the fish-kettle and stand it over a moderate fire to stew an hour and a half, according to the size; when done drain well, dress upon a dish without a napkin, and sauce over with a matelote sauce made as directed for salmon sauce matelote (No. 57), or caper sauce, as for skate (No. 74); small carp are very good-flavored, bread-crumbed and fried.

No. 80. *Truite à la Twickenham.* When you have cleaned your trout as described at page 23, put them into a kettle of boiling water, to which you have added a good handful of salt, and a wineglassful of vinegar; boil gently about twenty minutes, or according to their size, dress upon a napkin, and serve melted butter, into which you have put a tablespoonful of chopped gherkins in a boat.

The remains of trout, salmon, or mackerel are excellent pickled; put three onions in slices in a stewpan, with two ounces of butter, one turnip, parsley, thyme, and bay-leaf, pass them five minutes over the fire, add a pint of water and a pint of vinegar; boil until the onions are tender, then strain it through a sieve over the fish; it will keep some time if required, and then do to pickle more fish by boiling over again.

No. 81. *Truite à la Burton.* Boil the trout as in the last, then put half a pint of melted butter in a stewpan, with two tablespoonfuls of cream and two of milk, place it upon the fire, and when upon the point of boiling add a liaison of one yolk of egg mixed with a tablespoonful of cream (dress the fish upon a dish without a napkin), put two ounces of fresh butter, a pinch of salt, and the juice of a lemon into the sauce; shake round over the fire, but do not let it boil; sauce over the fish and serve.

No. 82. *Tench, Sauce Matelote.* Put three onions, a carrot, and turnip, cut in slices, into a stewpan, or very small fish-kettle, with a good handful of parsley, a few sprigs of thyme, three bay-leaves, six cloves, a blade of mace, a little salt, and two glasses of sherry; lay your tench over (it will require four for a dish, and they may be either cooked whole or each one cut into two or three pieces), add a pint of water, cover down close, and stew gently over a slow fire for about half an hour, take them out, drain upon a cloth, dress in pyramid upon a dish without a napkin, and pour a sauce over made as directed for salmon sauce matelote (No. 57), or as for stewed carp (No. 78).

No. 83. *Tench with Anchovy Butter.* Cook the tench as in the last, but they may be plain boiled in salt and water; dress upon a dish without a napkin, then put six spoonfuls of melted butter in a stewpan, with one of milk; place it upon the fire, and when upon the point of boiling add an ounce of anchovy butter (page 33), shake it round over the fire until the butter is melted, when sauce over and serve.

No. 84. *Perch fried in Butter.* Clean the fish as explained (p. 94), dry well, make an incision upon each side with a knife, put a quarter of a pound of butter in a sauté-pan over a slow fire, lay in the fish, fry gently, turning them over when half done; when done dress upon a napkin, and serve melted butter in a boat.

No. 85. *Perch, Hampton Court Fashion.* Cook the fish as above, and have ready the following sauce: put six spoonfuls of melted butter in a stewpan, with a little salt and the juice of a lemon; when upon the point of boiling stir in the yolk of an egg mixed with a tablespoonful of cream; do not let it boil; blanch about twenty small sprigs of parsley in boiling water ten minutes, drain and put them in the sauce, which pour over the fish and serve.

Perch may also be served plain boiled or stewed as directed for tench, with sauce served separate.

No. 86. *Eels Fried.* Cut your eels into pieces three inches long, dip the pieces into flour, egg over with a paste brush, and throw them into some bread-crumbs; fry in hot lard as directed for fried soles (p. 114).

No. 87. *Stewed Eels, Sauce Matelote.* Procure as large eels as possible, which cut into pieces three inches long, and put them into a stewpan, with an onion, two bay-leaves, a sprig of thyme and parsley, six cloves, a blade of mace, a glass of sherry, and two of water; place the stewpan over a moderate fire, and let simmer about twenty minutes, or according to the size of the eels; when done drain upon a cloth, dress them in pyramid upon a dish without a napkin, with a matelote sauce over, made as directed for salmon sauce matelote (No. 57), but using the stock your eels have been cooked in to make the sauce, having previously well boiled it to extract all the fat.

No. 88. *Gudgeons* are floured, egged, bread-crumbed, or simply floured and fried as directed for smelts; but being smaller, they require less time to cook.

No. 89. *Escaloped Oysters.* Put two dozen of oysters with their liquor into a stewpan, place over a fire, and when a little firm drain them upon a sieve, catching the liquor in another stewpan; detach the beard from the oysters, and throw them again into their liquor; add half a blade of mace, place again upon the fire, and when boiling add a piece of butter, the size of a walnut, with which you have mixed a teaspoonful of flour; shake round over the fire until becoming very thick, season with a little cayenne, and salt if required, have an escalop-shell, well buttered and bread-crumbed, place the oysters in, sprinkle bread-crumbs over, put it in the oven a quarter of an hour, pass the salamander over, and serve.

No. 90. *Stewed Oysters.* Blanch and beard the oysters as above, when done, put them with their liquor in a stewpan, with four cloves, a blade of mace, and a teaspoonful of essence of anchovies, with a little chopped parsley and cayenne; let simmer a minute, stir in two pats of butter, with which you have mixed half a teaspoonful of flour, let simmer a little longer, lay the oysters in your dish upon a piece of toast, and sauce over.

No. 91. *Gratin of Lobsters.* Procure a good-sized lobster, cut it in halves, detaching the head from the body, take out all the meat, and save the four shells; cut the meat into dice, then take a teaspoonful of chopped eschalots in a stewpan, with a piece of butter the size of two walnuts, pass them a few minutes over a fire, add a tablespoonful of flour (mix well in), half a pint of milk, stir over the fire, boiling about five minutes, then add the lobster, which season with a little cayenne, salt, chopped parsley, and essence of anchovies; stand it again upon the fire, stirring until boiling, then stir in the yolk of an egg; take off the fire, fill the shells of the lobster, sprinkle bread-crumbs over, put them into the oven about ten minutes, the top requiring to be browned; serve upon a napkin garnished with parsley.

SIMPLE HORS-D'ŒUVRES.

No. 92. *Rissoles of Oysters.* Prepare two dozen of blanched oysters as directed for escaloped oysters, but cutting each oyster into six pieces, turn it out upon a dish, where leave it until quite cold; then have the trimmings of some puff paste,[25] which roll very thin; put some of the oysters upon it in pieces the size of a walnut, fold them over with the paste, which cut out with a round cutter, giving each the shape of a turnover, egg with a paste brush, and throw them into bread-crumbs, cover well, have ready a stewpan in which there is some very hot lard or white dripping (as for frying fish), in which fry your rissoles of a light brown colour; dress upon a napkin in a plate, garnish with fried parsley, and serve to be handed round the table.

No. 93. *Rissoles of Lamb.* Cut up about a pound of cooked lamb (the remains of a previous day) into very small dice, with a quarter of a pound of lean cooked ham, then put a teaspoonful of chopped eschalots in a stewpan, with a piece of butter the size of a nut, pass them over the fire a couple of minutes, then stir in a teaspoonful of flour, after which add nearly half a pint of melted butter and the meat; stir it over the fire until it boils, season well with a little pepper and salt, and stir in the yolks of a couple of eggs, put it out upon a dish till cold, and proceed as directed in the last article.

The flesh of any poultry or game may be used exactly the same.

No. 94. *Rocambole, or Croquettes of Meat, Game, or Poultry.* Make a preparation as above with some description of cold cooked meat, or poultry; when cold divide it into pieces, each rather larger than a walnut, roll them to about two inches and a half in length, have three eggs in a basin well whisked, into which dip them, throw them into bread-crumbs, take them out, well covered, and smooth them by gently patting them with a knife, then dip them into clarified butter, and again into bread-crumbs, smooth them again, and fry them of a light colour in a stewpan of hot lard, and serve precisely the same as for rissoles.

No. 95. *Lamb's Fry.* See the other department of this work, page 312; nothing can be more simplified.

REMOVES SIMPLIFIED.

No. 96. *Stewed Rump of Beef.* Choose a small rump of beef, cut it away from the bone, cut about twenty long pieces of fat bacon, which run through the flesh in a slanting direction, then chop up the bone, place it at the bottom of a large stewpan, with six cloves, three onions, one carrot, a turnip, head of celery, a leek, and a bunch of parsley, thyme, and bay-leaf, then lay in the rump (previously tying it up with string), which just cover with water, add a good handful of salt and two burnt onions, place upon the fire, and when boiling stand it at the corner, let simmer nearly four hours, keeping it skimmed; when done pass part of the stock it was cooked in (keeping the beef hot in the remainder) through a hair sieve into a basin; in another stewpan have ready a quarter of a pound of butter, melt it over the fire, add six ounces of flour, mix well together, stirring over the fire until becoming a little brownish, take off, and when cold add two quarts of the stock, stir it over the fire until it boils, then have four carrots, four turnips (cut into small pieces with cutters), and forty button onions peeled, put them into the sauce, when again boiling draw it to the corner, where let simmer until tender, keeping it skimmed, add a little powdered sugar and a bunch of parsley; if it should become too thick add a little more of the stock, dress the beef upon a dish, sauce round and serve.

No. 97. *Stewed Rump of Beef with Onions.* See page 172, in the other department.

The remains of stewed beef, cut in slices and warmed in some of the stock, is good the next day served with a little sharp sauce (page 15). The remaining stock is good for any kind of soup or stock the next day.

No. 98. *Stewed Rump Steak with Oyster Sauce.* Cut from a small stale rump of beef two steaks, about-three quarters of an inch in thickness, season well with pepper and salt; well butter a deep sauté-pan, lay in your steaks, with four cloves, a blade of mace, and a bunch of parsley, thyme, and bay-leaf, cover with a quarter of a pint of water, set over a slow fire, when they have simmered half an hour turn them over, and let remain until quite tender; take up, place upon your dish, and keep them hot, place the sauté-pan at the corner of the fire, boil, skim well, add an ounce of butter, with which you have mixed half a tablespoonful of flour, stir well, and when it thickens add two dozen oysters previously blanched and bearded, half a teaspoonful of essence of anchovies, and a little cayenne pepper, sauce over the steaks and serve. The steak with common stewed oysters would be very good.

No. 99. *Ribs of Beef à l'Hôtelière.* Procure four ribs of beef, but not too fat or too thick, take off the chine-bone neatly, and the tips of the rib-bones, skewer the flap under, so as to form a good square piece; put a quarter of a pound of butter at the bottom of a large braising-pan, let melt, then lay in your beef (which must previously be larded through the best part with ten long pieces of fat bacon), seasoned with a teaspoonful of salt, and half ditto of pepper, cover the braising-pan, and put it upon a slow fire for twenty minutes, keeping it stirred round until becoming a nice gold colour, then add a pint of water; when about half done throw in eighty button onions and about sixty small pieces of carrot, cut the size and shape of young ones; half an hour after add the same number of pieces of turnips, and a bunch of parsley, to which you have added three bay-leaves and four sprigs of thyme, keep stewing gently until the vegetables are done, and the beef is quite tender, which take out, trim, and lay it upon your dish, skim off as much fat as possible from the vegetables, add an ounce of butter with which you have mixed a tablespoonful of flour, with a teaspoonful of sugar, boil altogether, dress round and serve.

No. 100. *Beef à la Mode.* The real beef à la mode is made as follows, and not as a kind of soup daily sold in cookshops.

Procure either a small piece of rump, sirloin, or ribs of beef, about twelve pounds in weight, take away all the bone, and lard it through with ten long pieces of fat bacon; then put it into a long earthen pan, with a calf's foot, four onions, two carrots cut in slices, if large, a bunch of parsley, two bay-leaves, two sprigs of thyme, two cloves stuck in one of the onions, half a teaspoonful of pepper, one of salt, four wineglasses of sherry, four ditto of water, and a pound of streaked bacon cut in squares, place the cover upon the pan, with a piece of common flour-and-water paste round the edges to keep it perfectly air-tight; put in a very moderate oven four hours, take out, place upon your dish with the vegetables and bacon round, skim the gravy, which pour over; but the above is best eaten cold, when it should not be taken out of the pan, nor the pan opened until nearly cold. A long brown earthen pan for the above purpose may be obtained at any china warehouse, but if you cannot obtain one, a stewpan must supply the place.

Another Method. Have ready six pounds of rump of beef cut into pieces two inches square, lard each piece through with two or three lardons of bacon; have also two pounds of streaked bacon, clear it from the skin, and cut it into squares half the size of the beef, put them into an earthen pan with two calf's feet (cut up), half a pint of sherry, two bay-leaves, a sprig of thyme, a bunch of parsley, four onions, with a clove in each, a blade of mace, and half a pint of water, cover the pan as in the last, and put it in a moderate oven for three hours; do not open the pan until three parts cold, then take out the meat, lay a little of the beef at the bottom of a stewpan (not too large), then a little of the bacon, then more beef, and so on alternately, press them together lightly, then pass the gravy through a hair sieve over, and leave it until quite cold, then dip the stewpan into hot water, and turn out upon your dish to serve; the calf's feet may be made hot in a little of the stock, to which add two pats of butter, with which you have mixed a teaspoonful of flour, a little chopped parsley, and half a spoonful of vinegar, and serve as an entrée. The above is excellent either hot or cold.

No. 101. *Ox-tongue.* Procure a well-pickled ox-tongue, if weighing five or six pounds it will take three hours gently boiling in a gallon of water; when done skin it and trim the root, serve where afterwards directed, or with spinach dressed as (No. 1088.)

No. 102. *Loin of Veal, with Stewed Celery.* Put a small loin of veal upon a spit surrounded with all descriptions of vegetables, tied up in oiled paper; roast, if a middling-sized one, about two hours and a half before a moderate fire, have sixteen heads of celery, trim off all the green part from the tops, and a little of the roots, wash well, then cover the bottom of a stewpan with slices of fat bacon, lay in the celery, two heads tied together, add two onions and a carrot, just cover them with a little good stock, made as directed for soupe Julienne (page 652), let simmer an hour or more until very tender, drain upon a cloth, untie them, dress the loin in the centre of your dish, make a border of the celery round, take out the bacon, onions, and carrot, skim off all the fat, reduce a little, add an ounce of butter, with which you have mixed half a tablespoonful of flour, stir well in, season with a little sugar, salt, and pepper, and when boiling, sauce over the celery and serve; add a little catsup and Harvey sauce to give a brownish colour to the sauce.

No. 103. *Loin of Veal, with White Sauce.* Roast a loin of veal as directed in the last, but keep it as white as possible, when done dress it upon your dish, with some small well-boiled cauliflowers round it, have a quart of white sauce made as directed (No. 136) boiling in a stewpan, sauce over the whole and serve; should peas be in season, a pint of young green ones may be boiled and sprinkled over.

No. 104. *Dress Fillet of Veal for Remove.* Procure a small fillet of veal, skewered up very round, and well covered with udder, place a good piece of streaked bacon in the centre where the bone was taken out, and stuff it under the udder thus: chop three quarters of a pound of beef suet very fine, which put into a basin with six ounces of bread-crumbs, the rind of half a lemon chopped very fine, a little grated nutmeg, two tablespoonfuls of chopped parsley, and a little chopped thyme and marjoram, with one bay-leaf, mixed, amalgamate the whole with the yolks of three, and two whole eggs, sew it in, surround your fillet when upon the spit with every description of vegetables, tie up in oiled paper, and roast about three hours before a moderate fire; when done clear it from the vegetables, skewer up with silver, plated, or polished skewers, draw out those it was first trussed with, place upon your dish with celery sauce (page 47), white sauce (No. 136), or rather thin melted butter, with which you have mixed two tablespoonfuls of Harvey sauce and one of catsup, and boiled until it becomes rather a clear brown sauce.

No. 105. *Breasts and Necks of Veal* may be plain roasted, or roasted in vegetables as above, and served with stewed peas (No. 1077), or a sauce jardinière (page 40), which are very simply described.

No. 106. *Half Calf's Head, with White Sauce.* Procure the half of a scalded calf's head, which put into a braising-pan, just cover with water, add a little salt, two onions, two carrots, two turnips, a large bunch of parsley, thyme, and bay-leaves, and six cloves; boil very gently for two hours, or until tender, which you can tell by pressing upon it with your finger; when done take up, drain and place in your dish, surrounded with some well-boiled potatoes cut in halves, and have ready the following sauce: put a pint and a half of melted butter into a stewpan, with the juice of a lemon, when boiling add two ounces of fresh butter and a pinch of salt, when the butter is melted add a liaison of two yolks of eggs, mixed with half a gill of cream, stir in quickly over the fire, but do not let it boil, sauce over and serve; the sauce requires to be rather highly seasoned.

Should you have the tongue and brains, boil the tongue with the head, when done skin it, lay the brains in warm water to disgorge, blanch them two minutes in boiling water, to which you have added a little salt and vinegar; skin, chop, and put them into a stewpan, with the juice of a lemon, a little pepper and salt, a tablespoonful of chopped parsley, and half a pint of melted butter, boil altogether a few minutes, turn out upon a dish, dress the tongue over, and serve with the calf's head.

No. 107. *Half Calf's Head in Currie.* Boil half a calf's head as directed in the last, and have ready the following sauce: put four large onions in slices in a stewpan, with two ounces of lean ham, three apples in slices, six cloves, a blade of mace, two bay-leaves, and two ounces of butter, pass them over the fire, until slightly browned, add two good tablespoonfuls of flour, and one of currie-powder, or a little more if required, mix well in, add a quart of the stock the head was boiled in, season with salt and sugar, reduce until of a proper consistency, rub it through a hair sieve or tammie, put into another stewpan, boil up, skim, and sauce over the head, which serve with rice, plain boiled, in a separate dish.

No. 108. *Half Calf's Head à la Vinaigrette.* (See No. 460, Kitchen of the Wealthy.)

No. 109. *Half Calf's Head Broiled, Sauce Piquante.* Boil the head as before, when done drain upon a napkin, place it upon a baking-sheet, egg over with a paste-brush, cover with bread-crumbs, put a few small pieces of butter upon it at various places, and put into a hot oven until well browned; dress upon your dish with a pint of good sharp sauce (page 15) round. The tongue and brains may be served dressed as described before, with each of the methods for dressing calf's head.

No. 110. *Large Veal Pie.* Have ready boiled a pound of streaked bacon, when cold cut it in large thin slices, also cut four pounds of lean veal from the fillet into large but thin slices, season each piece well with pepper and salt, and dip them into flour; lay some of the bacon at the bottom of a pie-dish, then some veal, over which sprinkle a little chopped eschalots, then more bacon, and so on alternately, finishing in a perfect dome; have ready a pound of half puff paste (p. 480), place a band round the edge of your dish, wet it, and pour in a quarter of a pint of water to the meat, cover with the remainder of the paste, egg over, and decorate it tastefully, bake an hour and three quarters in a moderate oven. They may also be made of the remains of a joint of veal previously served, but half a pint of white sauce (No. 136) used in it, and the water omitted, but the paste will then require to be much thinner, and it must be baked in a much warmer oven, or the meat would eat dry; a couple of bay-leaves in a veal pie is a great improvement.

No. 111. *Saddle of Mutton à la Bretonne.* (See page 189.)

No. 112. *Leg of Mutton basted with Devil's Tears.* Procure a fine but small leg of mutton which has been well kept, cut an incision in the knuckle, in which put a clove of garlic, rub all over with a spoonful of salt, a saltspoonful of cayenne, two ditto of black pepper, and another clove of garlic (well mixed), and let remain upon a dish until the following day, when place it upon a spit before a sharp fire, then procure about a quarter of a pound of fat bacon, place it upon a long toasting fork, running the prongs through the rind, and hold over the fire until in a blaze, then hold it over the mutton upon which it will drop in tears of fire, until all melted; it will give the mutton quite a peculiar flavour and appearance, and requiring a quarter of an hour less to roast than in the ordinary method; when done dress upon your dish, sauce over with two spoonfuls of Harvey sauce and serve.

No. 113. *Leg of Mutton, the Housewife's Method.* Have a good leg, beat it a little with a rolling-pin, make an incision in the knuckle, in which put two cloves of garlic, then put it into a braising-pan, with a pound of lean bacon cut in eight pieces, set over a moderate fire half an hour, moving it now and then until becoming a light brown colour, season with a little pepper and salt, add twenty pieces of carrots of the same size as the bacon, fifteen middling-sized onions, and when half done fifteen middling-sized potatoes, two bay-leaves, two cloves, and a pint of water, replace it upon a moderate fire, moving round occasionally, stew nearly three hours, dress upon your dish, with the carrots and onions dressed tastefully around, take off as much of the fat from the gravy as possible (which will be a little thickened by the potatoes), take out the bay-leaves, and pour the garniture round the mutton, which serve very hot.

No. 114. *Shoulder of Mutton, Savoyard's Method.* Put a small shoulder of mutton in a deep sauté-pan or baking-dish, season with a little pepper and salt, cover over with thin slices of fat bacon, then put in ten potatoes peeled and quartered, and the same quantity of apples, with half a pint of water, place in a moderate oven and bake for two hours, dress upon your dish, with the potatoes and apples round, skim all the fat from the gravy, which pour over and serve; it requires a little oil or butter over before baking.

No. 115. *Shoulder of Mutton à la Polonaise.* As described (No. 467) in the other department of this work.

No. 116. *Shoulder of Mutton, Provençale Fashion.* Roast a fine shoulder of mutton; whilst roasting mince ten large onions very fine, put them into a stewpan, with two tablespoonfuls of salad-oil, pass them ten minutes over a good fire, keeping it stirred, then add a tablespoonful of flour, stir well in, and a pint of milk, season with a little pepper, salt, and sugar; when the onions are quite tender, and the sauce rather thick, stir in the yolks of two eggs and take it off the fire; when the shoulder is done spread the onions over the top, egg over, cover with bread-crumbs, put in the oven ten minutes, and salamander a light brown colour, dress upon your dish, put the gravy from it in your stewpan, with a pat of butter, with which you have mixed a little flour, boil up, add a little scraped garlic, pour round the shoulder, which serve. The shoulder may also be dressed in the housewife's method, as directed for the leg. A little burnt sugar may be added.

No. 117. *Saddle of Lamb, Berlin Fashion.* Roast a small saddle of lamb an hour, keeping it rather pale; you have boiled eight or ten good potatoes, peel them, put in a stewpan, add two ounces of butter, a teaspoonful of salt, a quarter ditto of pepper, a tablespoonful of chopped parsley, and a little grated nutmeg; mix all well together with a fork, add half a gill of milk and one egg, turn well with a wooden spoon, let it get cold, and roll them in long shape and size of plover's eggs, egg and bread-crumb twice, fry light-coloured in hot lard or fat; dress your saddle upon a dish, surround it with the potatoes, have half a pint of melted butter in a stewpan, place upon the fire, and when upon the point of boiling stir in a quarter of a pound of maître d'hôtel butter (page 33) highly seasoned; when quite melted sauce round and serve with mint sauce likewise in a boat; for other variations see pages 197, 198, and following pages. Haunch, fore-quarter, or ribs may be dressed the same.

No. 118. *Leg or Shoulder of Lamb with Peas.* The leg or shoulder must be plain roasted (see page 645); boil a quart of very young peas, which strain and put into a stewpan, with a quarter of a pound of butter, half a teaspoonful of salt, and one of sugar, toss them well together over the fire until the butter is melted, when pour them into your dish and dress the joint over.

No. 119. *Leg or Shoulder, with French Beans.* Plain roasted as before; you have cut and boiled two hundred French beans, drain and put them into a stewpan with a quarter of a pound of fresh butter, a little pepper, salt, powdered sugar, and grated nutmeg, toss over the fire till the butter is melted, add half a pint of melted butter; boil altogether ten minutes, then stir in quickly a liaison of one yolk of egg mixed with a quarter of a gill of cream, pour them in your dish and serve the joint over.

No. 120. *Boiled Leg of Lamb, with Spinach.* Boil a small very white leg of lamb (see page 646), have also half a sieve of spinach, well picked, washed, and boiled, drain it quite dry, chop it very fine, and put it into a stewpan, with a quarter of a pound of fresh butter, a little salt, sugar, and grated nutmeg; stir over the fire until very hot, then add a tablespoonful of flour, eight of melted butter, and four of cream or milk, boil two or three minutes, keeping it stirred, then pour it upon your dish, and dress the leg over.

No. 121. *Neck of Lamb à la Jardinière.* Plain roast the neck; you have previously cut with a round tin cutter rather larger than a quill about fifty pieces of carrot, and one hundred pieces of turnip, half an inch in length, put them into a stewpan, with twenty button onions ready peeled, two ounces of butter, and a teaspoonful of powdered sugar; place them over a sharp fire (keeping them moved to prevent burning) ten minutes, add a tablespoonful of flour and a pint of broth, which reserve from your soup, stand it at the corner of the fire, add a small bunch of parsley, thyme, and bay-leaf and let boil until the vegetables are tender and the sauce becomes thickish, keeping well skimmed, then add a few ready boiled peas, French beans, Brussels sprouts, or any other green vegetables in season, pour the sauce in your dish, and dress the lamb upon it; if your sauce is not quite brown enough add a few drops of colouring to it.

No. 122. *Lamb's Head Broiled, with Mint Sauce, or Sauce Piquante.* Procure two heads, split them, but not to detach them, take out the brains and the greater part of the skull bone, forming each head as nearly as possible to the shape of a heart, put them into a braising-pan, with two onions, a carrot, turnip, head of celery, a bunch of parsley, thyme, and bay-leaf, six cloves, a blade of mace, and just cover them with a little water, stew them until quite tender, then take out, drain, egg over with a paste-brush, and cover them with bread-crumbs, place small pieces of butter here and there over them, place them in the oven ten minutes, then brown them with a salamander, and serve them with a good sauce piquante (page 15) round them, or they may be served with the brains cooked as directed for calf's brains (page 282) under them; sheeps' heads are done the same, only they require a longer time to stew.

The heart and pluck are also excellent served under them as follows: blanch them in boiling water twenty minutes, and when half cold cut the whole in very fine dice, put an ounce and a half of butter in a stewpan, with a spoonful of chopped onions, pass over the fire two minutes (keep stirring), then add a spoonful of flour (mix well), moisten with a pint of broth or milk, when boiling add the mince, and season with a teaspoonful of salt, a quarter ditto of white pepper, and a little grated nutmeg.

No. 123. *Loin or Neck of Pork à la Bourguinotte.* The neck or loin must be plain roasted; you have peeled and cut four onions in dice, put them into a stewpan, with two ounces of butter, stir over the fire until rather brown, then add a tablespoonful of flour, mix well, add a good pint of broth if any, or water, with an ounce of glaze, boil ten minutes, add two tablespoonfuls of French mustard, with a little pepper, salt, and sugar, pour the sauce upon the dish, and dress your joint upon it; serve with a little apple sauce separate in a boat.

No. 124. *Loin or Neck of Pork, Normandy fashion.* Procure a neck or loin, put it in a common earthen dish, having previously scored the rind, rub over with a little oil, place about twenty potatoes cut in halves or in quarters in the dish with the pork, ten onions peeled, and twenty apples peeled and quartered, place in a warm oven for an hour and a half or more, then dress it upon your dish with the apples, onions, and potatoes around, and serve.

No. 125. *Pig's Cheek, a new Method.* Procure a pig's cheek nicely pickled (see page 649), boil well until it feels very tender, tie half a pint of split peas in a cloth, put them into a stewpan of boiling water, boil about half an hour, take them out, pass through a hair sieve, put them into a stewpan, with an ounce of butter, a little pepper and salt, and four eggs, stir them over the fire, until the eggs are partially set, then spread it over the pig's cheek, egg with a paste-brush, sprinkle bread-crumbs over, place in the oven twenty minutes, brown it with the salamander and serve.

No. 126. *Sucking Pig* is merely plain roasted (see page 204), stuffed with sage and onions, but before putting it upon the spit it requires to be floured and rubbed very dry, otherwise the skin would not eat crisp; the usual method of serving it is to cut off the head, and divide the body and head of the pig in halves, lengthwise; serve apple sauce separate in a boat if approved of.

In my Kitchen at Home I can also roast a haunch or neck of venison, depending upon which is presented to me, and precisely as recommended in the other department of this book (page 222); for the remains I also proceed the same.

No. 127. *Roast Turkey.* Pluck, draw, and truss a turkey for roasting, stuff it at the breast with the same stuffing as directed for the fillet of veal (page 51); if it should weigh twelve pounds it will require two hours roasting before a strong fire, when done take it off the spit, take away the skewer and string it was trussed with, hold it by the legs, sprinkle a little salt over, and pour a little hot water or broth over the back to make a gravy,[26] and serve with broiled sausages, ham, or a piece of boiled bacon, separate.

No. 128. *Braised Turkey.* Truss a nice turkey with the legs inside as for boiling, then put three onions in slices at the bottom of a stewpan, with a carrot, turnip, leek, and a head of celery, also cut small, a bunch of parsley, a sprig of thyme, a bay-leaf, four cloves, a blade of mace, half a pound of lean ham, and two pounds of veal cut in dice, cover them with two quarts of water, then lay in the turkey, breast downwards, cover the stewpan close, and let it simmer about two hours over a slow fire; then take it up, place it upon your dish, with a cover over it to keep it hot, then pass the stock from it through a hair sieve into a stewpan, place it upon the fire, boil and skim off all the grease; then in another stewpan place two ounces of butter, let melt, then stir in a sufficient quantity of flour to make a roux, stir over the fire some time, but keeping it quite white, then take it off, stir until partly cold, add the stock, boil, keep it stirred; if too thick add a little milk, season with a little salt and sugar, place four cauliflowers nicely boiled round the turkey, sauce over the whole and serve; a boiled ham, tongue, or a piece of bacon is usually served separate with it.

No. 129. *Capons* or *Poulardes* are almost too extravagant for My Kitchen at Home, but may be either plain roasted or braised, as directed for the turkey in the last, and served with peas, French beans, or sauce jardinière, made as directed for the legs or shoulders of lamb, only for jardinière, stewing the vegetables in the sauce you have made from your braise, instead of the method there directed.

No. 130. *Fowls, with Mushroom Sauce.* Braise two fowls, trussed for boiling, precisely as directed for braised turkey; when your sauce is made, add a pottle of white button mushrooms, stew for half an hour in the sauce, adding a little sugar, then stir in a liaison of one yolk of egg mixed with a spoonful of cream, take it instantly from the fire, dress the poularde upon your dish, and sauce over.

No. 131. *Fowls, with Spring Vegetables.* Braise a poularde as directed for the turkey, and make a sauce from the braise as there directed; then have twenty young carrots and twenty young turnips, lightly peeled, and three parts boiled, with twenty small onions, drain and put them into your sauce, which you have made as No. 136, with a good teaspoonful of powdered sugar; stew them gently until tender, then dress the poularde upon your dish, arrange the vegetables tastefully around, mix half a gill of cream with the sauce, boil a few minutes, sauce over the whole and serve.

No. 132. *Fowls Braised, Fricassée Sauce.* Braise the fowls as before, and make the sauce from the braise, in which put a bunch of parsley, fifty button onions, and a pottle of mushrooms, both well peeled; stew half an hour, add a little sugar, salt, and a gill of cream, boil a few minutes, sauce over and serve. Chickens may be dressed in either of the above methods, calculating the time they require cooking by their size.

No. 133. *Roast Goose.* Pluck, draw, and truss a goose, fill the inside with sage and onions, by cutting four large onions into small dice, and put them into a stewpan with a few leaves of sage (chopped fine), and a couple of well-boiled mealy potatoes, crumbled very small, add two ounces of butter, and a little pepper and salt; when the onions become tender stuff the goose, the day previous if time permit, which roast an hour and a quarter before a moderate fire, serve plain, with a little gravy on the dish, and apple sauce separate.

No. 134. *Ducks* may also be stuffed and roasted as a goose; a few apples may also be used with the stuffing instead of potatoes, for either ducks or geese, if approved of.

No. 135. *Ducks à l'Aubergiste (or Tavern-keeper's fashion).* Truss one or two ducks with the legs turned inside, put them into a stewpan with a quarter of a pound of butter; place them over a slow fire, turning round occasionally, until they have taken a nice brown colour, add two spoonfuls of flour, mix well with them, add a quart of water, with half a tablespoonful of salt and sugar, let simmer gently until the ducks are done (but adding forty button onions well peeled as soon as it begins to boil), keep hot; peel and cut ten turnips in slices, fry them in a frying-pan with butter, drain upon a cloth, put them into the sauce, and stew until quite tender; dress the ducks upon your dish, skim the fat from the sauce, which has attained a consistency, pour round the ducks and serve.

SIMPLIFIED ENTRÉES.

The word entrée is a French culinary term (universally known by the nobility and gentry of Europe), signifying a corner, or made dish, in which sauce is introduced, the importance of which is known in the kitchens of the wealthy as forming the size and magnitude of a dinner. Being considered as the principal dish upon which it is intended to dine well, the wealthy epicure orders his cook to prepare a dinner of four, six, or eight entrées, thus making a criterion for the second course, which, in the opinion of real gourmets, is a secondary consideration of delight, and very often left entirely to the cook. But when a lady of moderate income is consulted, she very properly devotes all her attention, good taste, and economy to the subject.

The entrées, however, which I am here about to describe, are very economical; whilst those entrées of importance, which are so well known for their excellence and unavoidable expense, I have left to those whose means will better afford it, and content myself with here offering to my readers those only with which I would be content in placing before my friends at home.

My readers will find that certain made dishes, instead of being expensive, tend to greater economy. Every ordinary cook might be perfect in roasting and boiling a joint, but quite incapable of making a single made dish to perfection, even from the remains of a joint. In a tradesman's family it often happens that he dines once or twice a week from a Sunday joint, either in winter or summer; in the last it is partly excusable, but, in the former, hot meat for such an important meal is much more preferable, being more light than cold, and of course digests more freely. To prove the truth of this argument, pickles are continually used with cold meat to invigorate and open the appetite, and facilitate digestion. I would always advise to take a little cold lunch, and a hot late dinner, if circumstances permit, and *avoid* as much as possible a supper, particularly *a late one*.

SAUCES.—No. 136. For daily use I avoid making any foundation sauces, but when I want to give a little party at home, I generally previously provide a small quantity of white and brown sauce as follows:

Cut and chop a knuckle of veal, weighing about four pounds, into large dice; butter the bottom of a large stewpan with a quarter of a pound of butter, add two onions, a small carrot, a turnip, three cloves, half a blade of mace, a bay-leaf, a sprig of thyme, and six of parsley tied in a bunch; add a gill of water, place over a sharp fire, stirring round occasionally, until the bottom of the stewpan is covered with whitish glaze, when fill up with three quarts of water, add a good teaspoonful of salt, and let simmer at the corner of the fire an hour and a half, keeping well skimmed, when pass it through a hair sieve into a basin; in another stewpan put a quarter of a pound of butter, with which mix six ounces of flour, stirring over the fire about three minutes, take off, keep stirring until partly cold, when add the stock all at once, continually stirring and boiling for a quarter of an hour; add half a pint of boiling milk, stir a few minutes longer, add a little chopped mushrooms if handy, pass through a hair sieve into a basin, until required for use, stirring it round occasionally until cold; the above being a simplified white sauce.

For a brown sauce I use the same proportion as for the white, but having beef instead of veal for the stock, which must be made brown by placing four large onions cut in halves at the bottom of the stewpan, which must be well buttered, placing the meat over, standing upon the fire, and drawing down to a brown glaze before filling up; the thickening must also be made brown, by stirring a few minutes longer over the fire, and the milk omitted. Sometimes I make both stocks in the same stewpan, pass one half for the white sauce, and put a couple of burnt onions into the remainder, allowing it to simmer an hour longer, when pass and use for a brown sauce.

No. 137. *Melted Butter.* Put two ounces of butter into a stewpan, with which mix a good teaspoonful of flour, using a wooden spoon, add a saltspoonful of salt, half a one of pepper, a little grated nutmeg, and half a pint of water, stir over the fire until just upon the point of boiling, when take off, add two ounces more butter, and half a tablespoonful of vinegar, keeping it stirred until quite smooth, and the butter well melted, when pass through a hair sieve or tammie if required (you can also use milk instead of water for the above); it is then ready for use. In making melted butter great attention ought to be paid to the above directions, it being almost in daily use.

No. 138. *New and Economical Lobster Sauce.* Break up a fresh lobster, use the solid flesh for salad or any other purpose, pound the soft part and shell together (in a mortar) very fine, place the whole in a stewpan, cover with a pint of boiling water, place over the fire, and let simmer ten minutes, when pass the liquor through a hair sieve into a basin, and use for making melted butter as in the last, to which add a little cayenne pepper and a piece of anchovy butter (see page 33, Kitchen of the Wealthy) the size of a walnut; if any red spawn in the lobster, pound and mix it with a small piece of fresh butter, and add to the sauce with a little lemon-juice when upon the point of serving; an anchovy pounded with the shells of the lobster would be an improvement; some of the flesh may be served in the sauce.

No. 139. *Lobster Sauce à la Crème.* Cut up a small lobster into slices, the size of half-crown pieces, put into a stewpan, pound the soft and white part with an ounce of butter, and rub it through a sieve; pour three spoonfuls of melted butter, and two of cream, over the slices in the stewpan, add half a blade of mace, a saltspoonful of salt, a quarter ditto of pepper, and a little cayenne, warm gently, and when upon the point of boiling add the butter and two spoonfuls of thick cream, shake round over the fire until quite hot, when it is ready to serve.

No. 140. *Lobster Sauce simplified.* Put the slices of lobster as above into a stewpan, with four spoonfuls of milk, add a little salt, pepper, cayenne, two cloves, and a quarter of a blade of mace, let boil, add a piece of butter the size of a walnut, with which you have mixed a little flour, shake round over the fire, and when getting thick, add half a gill of cream; when quite hot it is ready to serve.

No. 141. *Shrimp Sauce* is very excellent made by pounding half a pint of shrimps with their skins, boiling ten minutes in three parts of a pint of water, finishing as directed for lobster sauce (No. 138), and always serving very hot.

No. 142. *Anchovy Sauce* is made by adding a spoonful of Harvey sauce and two of essence of anchovy, with a little cayenne, to half a pint of melted butter; shrimps, prawns, or even blanched oysters may be served in it.

No. 143. *Oyster Sauce.* Put two dozen of oysters into a stewpan with their liquor, and two spoonfuls of water, add six peppercorns, and half a blade of mace, blanch them until just set, drain the oysters upon a sieve, catching the liquor in another stewpan, detach the beards from the oysters, which put again into the liquor, place over the fire; when beginning to simmer, add a piece of butter the size of a walnut, with which you have mixed sufficient flour to form a paste, breaking it in four or five pieces, shake round over the fire, when it thickens add a gill of milk, season with a little cayenne, salt, pepper, and a few drops of essence of anchovies, serve very hot.

Another way. Blanch and save the liquor as above, omitting the water; reduce to half, add eight spoonfuls of melted butter made with milk, season rather high, adding a teaspoonful of Harvey sauce and one of essence of anchovy; it is then ready for use.

No. 144. *Caper Sauce.* Make half a pint of good melted butter, to which add a tablespoonful of capers and a teaspoonful of their vinegar. Observe, that all fish sauces are better too thick than too thin, the fish being watery, the sauce would not envelope it if too thin.

No. 145. *To chop Onions, Herbs, &c.* Every practical cook knows how to chop the above ingredients to perfection, but many plain cooks instead of chopping, literally smash them with their knives, thus losing the succulence and flavour, which becomes absorbed by the wood they are smashed upon.

For onions, peel, and cut in halves lengthwise, then with a thin knife cut each half in slices, leaving them jointed at the root; again cut into slices contrarywise, and then from top to bottom, thus having cut it into very small squares; then take the knife lightly with the right hand, place two fingers of the left upon the point, and commence chopping, lifting the knife entirely every stroke, not digging the point into the board, and pressing heavily upon the handle, as is too commonly the case; when chopped very fine put them into the corner of a clean cloth, which rinse in water to wash them, squeeze quite dry in the cloth, they will be then as white as possible, and quite ready for use. Eschalots are chopped in the same manner, cutting first into small dice, without cutting them in halves.

For parsley or herbs, previously wash very clean, take the stalks in your left hand (when quite dry), pressing upon the leaves with your fingers, holding the knife with your right hand, cutting as fine as possible; chop as directed for the onions. By following the above directions you will be enabled to chop them very fine, scarcely staining the board; the above directions to some may appear superfluous, but the difference made in the flavour of sauces, by their being well or badly chopped, being so great, caused me to make these observations.

No. 146. *To make a Colouring or Browning from Sugar.* Put two ounces of white powdered sugar into a middling-sized stewpan, which place over a slow fire; when beginning to melt, stir round with a wooden spoon until getting quite black, when set it in a moderate oven upon a trivet about twenty minutes, pour a pint of cold water over, let dissolve, place in a bottle, and use wherever directed in My Kitchen at Home.

ECONOMICAL MADE DISHES.

No. 147. *Fillet of Beef* or a small rump steak is very excellent dressed in the following new way:

Procure a piece of fillet of beef, weighing from three to four pounds, which can be purchased in any butcher's shop, being the under part of the rump; trim it a little, taking off part of the skin, leaving a piece of fat half an inch in thickness upon each side, cut it crosswise in slices a quarter of an inch in thickness, making about six pieces, beat lightly, giving them a roundish shape; place them upon a gridiron over a sharp fire, season whilst broiling with about a saltspoonful of salt, and the half of one of black pepper, turn them once or twice whilst upon the gridiron, which process will keep the gravy in, and when done dress them immediately upon a dish, in which you have put the following simple but excellent sauce, which I usually make over an ordinary fire; put the yolks of four eggs in a stewpan or iron saucepan, with half a pound of fresh butter (rather firm) cut into slices, half a teaspoonful of salt, a quarter ditto of pepper, the juice of half a lemon, and half a tablespoonful of chopped parsley; set upon a slow fire, keep stirring quickly with a wooden spoon in every direction, until becoming rather thick, when remove it from the fire half a minute, still stirring, then again upon the fire, stirring until the butter is quite melted, but congealed with the yolks of eggs, forming a smooth thickish sauce; should it, however, be too thick, add a little milk or cream, and if requiring more seasoning add a little pepper and salt, with the juice of the other half lemon; proceed the same for rump steak, but if for a corner dish, the fillet would be preferable, as the steak would be too large, appearing clumsy. The above quantity would be sufficient for a party of ten, but a much smaller quantity might be made.

A great improvement would be to have four or five middling-sized potatoes, peeled, cut in quarters lengthwise, and afterwards into thin slices crosswise; have ready upon the fire a stewpan, containing lard or dripping, when hot (which you may perceive by the smoke arising from it, or by throwing a drop of water in, if sufficiently hot it will hiss and snap), put in the slices of potatoes, and fry about ten minutes until crisp, and a very light brown colour; care must be taken that the fat is not too hot, or the potatoes would be burnt before they were sufficiently cooked.

Another method of frying potatoes, although rather more extravagant, is very simple and excellent: put a quarter of a pound of butter in a stewpan or saucepan, and when melted put in twenty small new potatoes, if in season, or potatoes cut as before, place over a sharp fire, stirring them occasionally, until of a nice gold colour; should they absorb all the butter, add a little more, when done sprinkle a little salt over, and serve round the fillet or steak; this may be used in many instances in the kitchens of the wealthy.

No. 148. *A new Steak.* Procure a piece of ribs of beef containing a couple of bones, from which detach the meat, and cut three steaks lengthwise, beat lightly with the cutlet-bat, trim a little, broil one or two, seasoning them well, and serve with sauce and fried potatoes as before.

No. 149. *Fillet* or *Steak à la Maître d'Hôtel.* Cut, trim, and broil the fillet or steaks, from either the rump or ribs of beef, as before (always over a sharp fire); place them upon your dish, have ready two ounces of butter, with which you have mixed a saltspoonful of salt, a quarter ditto of white pepper, one of chopped parsley, and the juice of half a lemon, rub all over the steaks, turning them three or four times, the butter mixing with the gravy forms an admirable sauce; serve with fried potatoes round as before.

The above steaks or fillets are also very excellent broiled as above, and served with anchovy butter (page 33), instead of the butter prepared as last directed, and using one ounce instead of two.

Should any of the above steaks be required plain broiled, to give them an extra zest, sprinkle chopped eschalots in addition to the other seasoning over previous to placing them upon the gridiron; a steak cut of the ordinary size, would require ten minutes broiling over a good fire. Mutton and lamb chops, or even cotelettes, are very good dressed in the before-mentioned manners; a little glaze, if handy, is also an improvement. For mutton chops, a little Harvey sauce and Chili vinegar poured over just before taking from the gridiron renders them very beautiful eating.

No. 150. *A new Mutton or Lamb Chop.* Having previously and successfully introduced a new joint (the saddle-back), I thought I would also introduce a new form of mutton or lamb chops, and adopted the following one, as represented in the engraving, which is not only very novel, but the manner in which the chops are cut, by jagging the meat, causes them to eat much lighter and better, they being sawed off the saddle instead of cut from the loin; proceed as follows:

Trim a middling-sized saddle of mutton, which cut into chops, half an inch in thickness, with a saw, without at all making use of a knife; then trim to the shape represented in the drawing; season well with salt and pepper, place upon a gridiron over a sharp fire, turning them three or four times, they will require about ten minutes cooking; when done place them upon a dish, spread a small piece of fresh butter (if approved of) over each, and serve. The bone keeping the gravy in whilst cooking, is a very great advantage in having chops cut after the above method. At home, when I have a saddle of mutton, I usually cut three or four such chops from it, cook and rub maître d'hôtel butter over, and serve them with fried potatoes round, using the remainder of the saddle as a joint the next day.

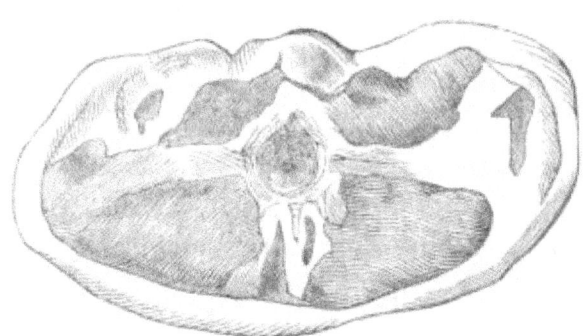

The above are also excellent seasoned, dipped into eggs, and bread-crumbed previous to broiling; for lamb chops proceed precisely the same, only broiling them a few minutes less.

No. 151. *Veal Cutlets.* Cut four cutlets from the neck, half an inch in thickness, beat lightly with a chopper, and cut off the chine-bones, season them well; have a couple of eggs well beaten upon a plate, into which dip them, then into bread-crumbs, take out, pat gently with a knife, and broil rather more than ten minutes upon a gridiron over a good fire, turning occasionally, keening them of a very light brown colour; dress upon a dish, spreading a piece of the maître d hôtel butter over each, turning them two or three times in the dish, and serving very hot. Veal cutlets are also very good served with the new sauce as for fillets of beef or steaks, and the fried potatoes around them.

No. 152. *Pork Chops.* Take four chops from a loin of pork, each about half an inch in thickness, beat them lightly, trim, season well with pepper and salt, broil nearly a quarter of an hour over a good fire, and serve very hot upon a dish, with or without apple-sauce in a boat.

No. 153. *Pork or Veal Chops Fried.* Put one ounce of butter in a sauté or frying-pan, rub over the bottom, lay in four chops, well seasoned as in either of the last two; place the pan over a moderate fire, when the chops become coloured upon one side turn them over, they will require turning two or three times before done; when done, and of a nice colour, take them out, and place upon a dish; put a spoonful of chopped onions in the pan, which fry until becoming of a brownish colour, then take off as much of the fat as possible, add a teaspoonful of flour (mix well with a wooden spoon), and moisten with half a pint of water; stir quickly, add a bay-leaf, and when boiling season with half a saltspoonful of pepper, two of salt, one of sugar, and two spoonfuls of vinegar, stir over the fire until forming a sauce, when again lay in the chops, let simmer five minutes, dress the chops upon a dish, add two chopped gherkins to the sauce, which pour over and serve; a little brown colouring (No. 146) added to the sauce would improve their appearance.

No. 154. *Hashed Beef* is made from any description of roast beef. It may also be made from stewed, but roast is preferable. Cut about a pound and a half of meat into thin slices, using a small quantity of the fat; lay them upon a dish, sprinkle a spoonful of flour, a teaspoonful of salt, and a quarter ditto of pepper, place the meat in a stewpan, moisten with half a pint of water or light broth, if handy; add a little colouring (No. 146) to give a nice brown colour, place it upon the fire, allowing it to warm gently, stirring occasionally, simmering a quarter of an hour, taste if requiring more seasoning, if so add a little and serve very hot immediately. In making a hash of any description, avoid having to keep it hot as much as possible, or it would become greasy, and likewise prevent the hash boiling over the fire, which would cause the meat to eat hard and tough. If the beef has been well roasted, as described (page 639), the remainder, being underdone, makes an excellent and very nutritious hash.

To vary any description of hash, it may be served upon a large piece of buttered toast, or half a spoonful of chopped onions may be added with the flour and seasoning; chopped parsley may also be added with a spoonful of catsup, two of Harvey sauce, two of vinegar, or one of Chili vinegar; four nice green gherkins in slices may also be added at the time of serving. Some fresh mushrooms from the fields, cleaned, and stewed in the hash, is also a great improvement, a bay-leaf also added imparts a pleasant flavour. A little meat left upon the bones, well peppered and broiled, are frequently served with the hash.

No. 155. *Remains of Salt Beef*, although very good cold, in winter is very desirable made hot; one of the best methods of doing which is to convert it into that old-fashioned dish entitled bubble-and-squeak; the beef should be, as usual, rather underdone, and cut into slices not thicker than a five-shilling piece, then put two ounces of butter in a sauté or frying-pan, when melted lay in the beef, which place over a quick fire, frying both sides of a yellowish brown colour, when take them out upon a dish, keeping them hot; you have previously boiled six or eight greens or one Savoy cabbage, which chop fine, season with four saltspoonfuls of salt and one of black pepper, place in the same pan you fried the beef in over the fire, keep turning them over until quite hot, when dress upon a dish with the beef over, and serve. A few slices of fat ought to be fried with the beef.

Another way of warming salt beef, is to cut slices and lay in a pan with just sufficient water to cover them; place over the fire, add about an ounce of fresh butter mixed with a little flour, a little Harvey sauce, and a piece of glaze about the size of a walnut, if handy. Another way would be to lay the slices in a saute or frying-pan well buttered, place over the fire and fry a light brown colour, pour off as much of the fat as possible, add a quarter of a pint of water, and a piece of butter the size of a walnut, with which you have mixed half a teaspoonful of flour, shake round over the fire a minute or two, add two spoonfuls of piccalilly cut in slices, two ditto of the liquor, and one of the colouring (No. 146), and serve over when ready.

No. 156. *Ox Tails en Currie*. Have ready some ox tails dressed as described in page 273 (they will keep several days in a basin covered with their own stock), when wanted warm them in their stock, cut four onions into very thin slices, put them into a stewpan with a quarter of a pound of butter, fry over a slow fire until the onions become brown and pulpy, when add a nicely boiled mealy potato (peeled), a tablespoonful of currie-powder, and one of currie-paste, or one and a half of the powder, mix all well together, moisten with three parts of a pint of the stock from the tails; then add the tails, stirring them round gently until well covered with the sauce, set over a slow fire to stew very slowly for half an hour, moving them round occasionally, finish with a little salt and the juice of half a lemon; dress upon a dish pyramidically, pour the sauce, which must be rather thick, over, and serve with rice boiled as directed (page 51) upon a separate dish.

Another way, for a change, would be to introduce four very ripe tomatas at the same time with the potato and currie-powder, omitting the lemon-juice, and adding half a teaspoonful of sugar. A tablespoonful of currie-paste added to any description of hash would convert it into a very good currie.

No. 157. *Ragout of Ox Tails.* Cut two ox tails into pieces two inches in length, rub two ounces of butter over the bottom of a convenient-sized stewpan, place in the pieces of tails, with half a pound of streaked bacon cut into square pieces the size of walnuts, place over a moderate fire, stirring occasionally until nicely browned, but not in the least burnt, add two ounces of flour (mix well) and three pints of water; when boiling and half cooked add a bunch of parsley, with two bay-leaves, twenty young carrots, or pieces of old ones, and twenty button onions, season with a teaspoonful of salt, a half ditto of sugar, and a quarter ditto of pepper; let simmer until the tails and vegetables are quite tender, keeping well skimmed, when take out and dress them in pyramid upon mashed potatoes, garnish round with the vegetables, pass the sauce through a hair sieve into another stewpan, place over the fire, stir with a wooden spoon until adhering to the back, when pour over the tails, and serve very hot.

No. 158. *Ox Cheeks* are very delicate when well stewed, and may be purchased very cheap; they require soaking all night, and about six hours to blanch in salt water, until the flesh will detach easily from the bone, when take it out, remove the bone, place some onion, carrot, and turnip, in slices, in a large flat stewpan, with a piece of bacon, a few sprigs of thyme, parsley, and two bay-leaves, cover with a little stock (if any) or water, place the flesh from the cheek over, put in a moderate oven until very tender, when take up, dress upon a dish, and serve with a sharp sauce over.

Ox cheeks may also be served in currie, or converted into a ragout after blanching, as directed for ox tails.

Should you happen to have the remains of a fresh ox tongue, it would be very good cut in slices, warmed, and served with a sharp sauce, or hashed; the remains of a pickled one may be used in any little made dish of veal, or poultry, hereafter described; to some persons it is, however, preferable cold.

No. 159. *Ox Kidneys* are very good for breakfast or luncheon; cut the kidneys into thin slices, avoiding the piece in the centre, put two ounces of butter in a stewpan, with a little chopped eschalots, place over the fire; when becoming a little browned add the kidneys, which keep stirring for five minutes still over the fire, add half a tablespoonful of flour (mix well), two glasses of sherry, two of water, half a teaspoonful of salt, a quarter ditto of pepper, one of chopped parsley, and a bay-leaf, let simmer gently five minutes, not, however, to boil, or they would become hard and indigestible; should the sauce be too thin add a little butter and flour mixed together, it requires to be sufficiently thick to envelope the kidneys; when done poor out upon a dish, and serve very hot. A few raw mushrooms stewed with the kidneys is also a great improvement.

A bullock's heart is a favorite dish with some persons; soak an hoar in lukewarm water to disgorge, dry, and stuff the interior with a good veal stuffing, roast an hour and a half before a moderate fire, and serve very hot, with a little veal sauce (see page 647) around; proceed the same for calves' or sheep's hearts, but of course they will require less time.

No. 160. *Calf's Head.* Should you have any left from a previous dinner it may be dressed in various ways. To hash calf's head, cut into good slices not too thin, or it would have a bad appearance; put a spoonful of chopped onions in a stewpan, with a wineglassful of vinegar, six peppercorns, a sprig of thyme, a bay-leaf, a piece of glaze the size of a walnut, and a gill of broth, reduce to half over the fire, then add the slices of calf's head and a gill more broth, season with a little pepper and salt, when quite hot through add half an ounce of butter, with which you have mixed a tablespoonful of flour, first breaking it into four or five pieces, shake round over the fire until becoming a little thickish, add a little colouring (No. 146) to give a light brown colour; pour out upon your dish, and serve with a few slices of gherkins sprinkled over.

Calf's head may also be cut in slices, warmed, and served with some of the sauces as directed for fillet of beef, or curried as for the ox-tails (No.

156); hashed calf's head, with a couple of spoonfuls of currie-paste added, is also very excellent.

No. 161. *Calf's Brains and Tongue.* Boil the tongue in stock or water until tender, lay the brains in lukewarm water to disgorge, then carefully take off all the skin, put about a quarter of a pound of butter in a sauté-pan, rub all over the bottom, cut the brains in slices, lay them in the pan, season with a little pepper, salt, and lemon-juice, place over a moderate fire, and when set turn them over, add about a gill of melted butter, and a little milk, if too thick, season a little more if required, shake the sauté-pan round, moving the brains from the bottom, but not breaking them, and pour upon a dish, skin and trim the tongue, cut it in halves lengthwise, glaze and serve dressed upon the brains. Sheep and lamb's tongues and brains are dressed in precisely the same manner as the calf's.

No. 162. *Veal Cutlets, the English Method.* Procure a piece of fillet of veal weighing about four pounds, from which (to the best advantage) cut eight or ten pieces of the shape and size of fillets of fowl, season lightly with a little pepper and salt, have a couple of eggs, well beaten, upon a plate, into which dip the cutlets, and afterwards into bread-crumbs, beat lightly; then cut four or five slices of streaked bacon, which fry in a sauté or frying-pan; when done take out and lay in the cutlets, which fry of a nice light brown colour, dress the bacon and cutlets alternately upon your dish, pour as much fat as possible out of the pan, into which pour a quarter of a pint of water, and the same of melted butter; boil until becoming rather thickish, when add a tablespoonful of Harvey sauce, one of catsup, a little colouring (No. 146), and a little pepper and salt, boil another second, pass through a sieve over the cutlets, and serve. Veal cutlets cut and fried as above may also be served upon some very light mashed potatoes, omitting the sauce.

No. 163. *Sweetbreads.* I never can procure sweetbreads at home except in the autumn or winter season of the year, so many families being then out of town, they may be procured at a very reasonable price; I usually dress them thus: lay them in water three or four hours to disgorge, blanch two minutes in boiling water, take out and put them into another stewpan, with a few slices of onions, carrot, turnip, a little parsley, thyme, bay-leaf, six peppercorns, a blade of mace, and a small piece of bacon, cover over with a little broth if any, place over the fire, and let boil about twenty minutes, then take out, dry them on a cloth, egg all over, throw into bread-crumbs, run a skewer through each, tie them to a spit and roast of a nice brown colour before a sharp fire, a quarter of an hour would be sufficient; they might also be browned in a hot oven, or fried in very hot lard or dripping ten minutes; then, however, they must be stewed rather longer; serve them with vegetable garniture of any description, if peas, merely plain boiling them, putting them in a stewpan, with a little sugar, pepper, salt, and a piece of fresh butter, toss them round over the fire until very hot, pour them into the dish, and dress the sweetbreads over, or serve with French beans dressed also in the same manner, spinach dressed as directed (page 43), or merely with the following sauce: put a gill of melted butter into a stewpan, with a spoonful of Harvey or Reading sauce, and a little catsup, boil altogether, and if too thick add a little water. If I cannot meet with heart sweetbreads, I in general satisfy myself with the throats.

No. 164. *Calf's Liver Stewed, French fashion.* Procure a small delicate liver, cut twenty pieces of fat bacon, three inches in length and a quarter of an inch square, season with a little pepper, salt, and chopped parsley, then with a larding-needle run them into the liver crosswise, put two ounces of butter into a convenient-sized stewpan, with half a pound of lean uncooked ham, keep stirring over a sharp fire until the ham becomes rather brownish, then lay in the liver, cover the stewpan, stir round occasionally until the liver has become quite firm and of a brownish colour; then add half a teaspoonful of salt, a quarter of one of pepper, forty button onions, twenty young carrots (or twenty pieces of old, previously blanched), half a pint of water, a bunch of parsley, with three sprigs of thyme and two bay-leaves (tied together), four cloves, and a blade of mace, let simmer twenty minutes; then add twenty new potatoes, or old ones cut of the same size, cover the stewpan, and let stew gently until all the vegetables are done, when take out the bunch of herbs, dress the liver upon a dish, with the vegetables and ham around it, skim all the fat from the gravy in the stewpan, pour over the vegetables and serve; if any remain, it is excellent made hot the next day, or even to be eaten cold.

No. 165. *Calf's Liver Fried.* Cut the liver into slices the eighth of an inch in thickness, dip them in flour, and fry them in a sauté or frying-pan, in which you have previously fried some slices of streaked bacon, fry the liver until quite browned and rather crisp, when take out and place it upon a dish with the bacon, pour as much of the fat as possible from the pan, pour in a quarter of a pint of water, when boiling add a piece of butter the size of a walnut, with which you have mixed a teaspoonful of flour, shake the pan round over the fire until becoming rather thickish, season with a little Harvey sauce, catsup, pepper, and salt, if too thick add a little more water, pour over the liver and serve. Or, for variation, after the liver is well fried, take it out and put a tablespoonful of chopped onions in the pan, set upon the fire a minute, then pour off the greater part of the fat, add a teaspoonful of flour, mix well in, and half a pint of broth or water, boil until forming a thickish sauce, season with pepper, salt, two spoonfuls of vinegar, a little sugar, and half a teaspoonful of mixed mustard, set upon the fire until quite hot, pour over the liver and serve. Or liver may be served plain fried with bacon, without any sauce whatever. Sheep or lamb's liver may be dressed precisely in the same manner.

With the remains of a joint of veal, either roasted, boiled, or braised, I make mince, hashes, blanquettes, and even pies. For a blanquette of veal cut about a pound into thin slices of the size of half-crown-pieces, add also a few slices of cooked tongue, ham, or streaked bacon, season well with about a teaspoonful of chopped onions, half ditto of salt, and a quarter ditto of white pepper, add a gill of broth or water, warm gently, and when quite hot add a piece of butter the size of a walnut, with which you have mixed a teaspoonful of flour, shake round over the fire, when becoming thickish add half a gill of milk or cream, with which you have mixed the yolk of an egg, stir in quickly, add the juice of half a lemon, and serve (it must not boil after the egg and cream have been added) with triangular pieces of toasted or fried bread round. A blanquette of lamb made in the same manner is equally good. With the bones you may make a little stock by chopping them up into small pieces, and putting them into a stewpan, with an onion in slices, a bay-leaf, bunch of parsley, and a little raw ham, add water according to the quantity of bones, and boil rather more than half an hour, convert it into sauce by thickening with a little butter and flour, and use for hash; to make which cut the meat into small thin slices, put into a stewpan, with sufficient of the above sauce to moisten it, let simmer ten minutes, add two spoonfuls of vinegar and four gherkins in slices, season with a little white pepper and salt; pour upon your dish and serve.

No. 166. *Minced Veal and Poached Eggs* are also a very favorite dish; from the remains of veal cut about a pound of the lean, with a little of the fat, and two ounces of cooked ham into very small dice, put a tablespoonful of chopped onions into a stewpan, with half an ounce of butter, place over the fire, keep stirring until the onions change colour slightly, then stir in a tablespoonful of flour, moisten with half a pint of stock or milk, let boil ten minutes, add the mince, season well with white pepper and salt, when quite hot stir in a yolk of egg, mixed with two tablespoonfuls of cream or milk, do not let boil afterwards, finish with the juice of half a lemon, and pour upon your dish; have ready poached six eggs, by having a stewpan upon the fire with one quart of water, quarter of an ounce of salt, and a quarter of a gill of vinegar, when boiling break in six eggs separately, let boil from three to four minutes, draw off the fire, take them out with a colander spoon, drain a moment upon a cloth, dress upon the mince, pour a little melted butter over each, and serve with triangular pieces of fried bread round.

Minced lamb, beef, or mutton is done the same, using stock or water instead of milk, and letting the onions with the thickening become a little brown over the fire, likewise omit the yolk of egg and cream, serve with the eggs precisely the same; any kind of mince must be rather thick that the eggs may rest on it. By finishing the minced veal with the yolks of three eggs, stirring a moment over the fire until set, and pouring upon a dish until cold, you can serve it in any shaped croquettes you please, taking pieces from it of the size you may require, shaping them with a knife, dipping twice into eggs and bread-crumbs, patting them gently, frying a light brown colour in a stewpan of hot lard or dripping, and serving upon a napkin garnished with fried parsley; they may be made in oblong shapes, the size and length of small sausages, and fried as above: they are then called boudins.

Patties may also be made from cooked veal, preparing a blanquette as before described, and leaving it upon a dish until cold; line six large patty-pans very thinly with half puff paste (see page 480), lay some of the veal in the centre of each, sprinkle a little water over, and cover with sheets of the same paste of the thickness of a five-shilling piece, egg over, crimp the edges a little with a knife, place a leaf of paste upon the top of each, and bake about twenty minutes in a very hot oven until the paste is well done.

The remains of poultry, game, or any other description of meat, may also be converted into patties in the same method as above.

The remains of meat dressed as for the above patties is also very excellent for larger pies, filling the dish with it, when cold covering with paste, and baking in a rather warm oven.

No. 167. *Mutton Cutlets Sautés.* Cut eight cutlets from a neck of mutton, as directed (page 294), and put them into a sauté-pan, with an ounce of butter, season well with pepper and salt, place over the fire, when becoming a little browned turn them over, when firm to the touch they are done (which will take about ten minutes); take up and dress them upon your dish, pour as much of the fat as possible from the pan, add a quarter of a pint of water or broth, let boil until becoming a thin glaze, add a little sugar and a spoonful of Harvey sauce, pour over the cutlets and serve. Should you want a thick sauce you can obtain it by adding a small piece of butter, with which you have mixed a little flour, to the gravy in the sauté-pan, adding also a little colouring (No. 146).

No. 168. *Mutton Cutlets Sautés, with Vegetables.* Dress the cutlets as in the last, have some vegetables of all kinds (that is, carrots, turnips, artichokes, and button onions), cut up small, stew them in a little broth with a little sugar until tender, when pour them into the sauté-pan you cooked the cutlets in, reduce until the stock becomes a thin glaze, then dress the vegetables in the centre of the cutlets, sauce over, and serve.

No. 169. *Mutton Cutlets, Irish Method.* Cut eight or ten mutton cutlets, season well with pepper and salt, place them in a stewpan, just cover them with water, let simmer gently twenty minutes, then add forty button onions, and as many pieces of potatoes, cut with a scoop in pieces a size larger; stew until tender, dress the cutlets in a circle upon your dish, with the vegetables in the centre, skim off some of the fat from the stock in the sauté-pan, reduce a little, sauce over, and serve.

No. 170. *Mutton Cutlets Broiled.* Cut eight or ten cutlets, season well with pepper and salt, dip them into eggs, then into bread-crumbs, beat gently with a knife, have a little butter in a stewpan, which melt over the fire; dip each cutlet into the butter, and again into bread-crumbs, beat again lightly, place them upon a gridiron over a moderate fire; when lightly coloured upon one side turn them over; they will require about ten minutes to cook thoroughly; serve plain dressed upon your dish.

Dressed as above they may likewise be served with a maître d'hôtel sauce made thus: put half a pint of melted butter into a stewpan with a piece of glaze the size of a walnut, when boiling add two ounces of maître d'hôtel butter (see p. 33), shake the stewpan round over the fire; when quite hot pour in the dish with the cutlets, have ready some thin slices of potatoes fried as for the fillet of beef, dress in pyramid in the centre, and serve.

No. 171. *Mutton Cutlets Harricoed.* Cut ten cutlets from a neck of mutton, leaving them rather short, not beating them flat, and taking off some of the fat; put two ounces of butter in a stewpan, lay in the cutlets, which well season with pepper and salt; set upon a moderate fire, turning them round occasionally until of a lightish brown colour, then add a good spoonful of flour; mix well, and moisten with a quart of water, keep stirring until boiling, throw in twenty small onions, twenty small pieces of carrots, and the same of turnips (each about the size of walnuts), and a small bunch of parsley, with two bay-leaves; let simmer until the vegetables are done, skim well, take out the cutlets, which dress in crown upon a dish, place the vegetables in the centre, reduce the sauce if required, which pour over and serve. Should it be convenient, it would be as well to pass the vegetables by putting about a quarter of an ounce of powdered sugar into a stewpan; place over the fire, and when melted add two ounces of butter and the vegetables, which keep tossing over the fire until covered with a kind of glaze, when put them into the stewpan with the cutlets; it gives the harrico quite a peculiar and good flavour.

No. 172. *Ragout of Mutton en Currie.* Peel and slice four large onions, which put into a stewpan with two ounces of butter, place over a moderate fire, and when becoming lightly browned and pulpy lay in ten cutlets as in the last; move round occasionally until a little brown, when add a good spoonful of currie-powder and the half of one of flour; mix well, moisten with a pint of water, let simmer twenty minutes, or until the mutton is quite tender, finish with a little sugar, salt, and lemon-juice, take out the cutlets, which dress in circle upon a dish, have ready some boiled rice (p. 51) very hot, which dress in pyramid in the centre; pass the sauce through a tammie, pour over the cutlets, and serve.

No. 173. *Mutton Currie.* Peel and slice four large onions as in the last, fry the same, have ready two pounds of lean mutton cut into square pieces the size of walnuts, put into the stewpan with the fried onions; let remain ten minutes over the fire, stirring frequently, then add a tablespoonful of currie-powder and one of currie-paste; mix well in, let remain over a slow fire until the mutton is tender, season with a little salt and lemon-juice, pour out upon your dish, and serve with boiled rice separate.

Lamb cutlets are dressed precisely as the mutton; but when breadcrumbed and broiled they are very good served with peas or French beans, previously boiled, and placed in a stewpan with an ounce of fresh butter, a little pepper, salt, and sugar; when quite hot stir in half a gill of cream, with which you have well mixed the yolk of an egg, stir in quickly, pour out upon your dish, dress the cutlet over, and serve.

No. 174. *Pork Cutlets Sautés.* Cut six or eight good-sized cutlets from the neck, of the same shape as the mutton, lay them in a buttered sauté-pan, season well with pepper and salt, place over the fire; when done lay them upon a plate, pour some of the fat from the sauté-pan, add a good tablespoonful of chopped onions, pass over the fire a minute, then add a teaspoonful of flour; moisten with half a pint of broth or water, with a piece of glaze added, season a little more, add a bay-leaf and a teaspoonful of vinegar, with one of mustard, mix well, lay in the cutlets until quite hot, when dress upon a dish, sauce over, and serve. This sauce is good with any kind of cutlets, but especially pork.

No. 175. *Pork Cutlets aux Cornichons.* Cut six or eight cutlets from a middling-sized neck of pork, season well with pepper and salt, dip in eggs well beaten upon a plate, and then into grated crust of bread (not too brown); put two ounces of lard or butter into a sauté or frying-pan, lay in the cutlets and fry very slowly; when done place them upon a dish; keep hot, pour some of the fat from the pan, add a good teaspoonful of flour, mix well, moisten with half a pint of broth or water with a piece of glaze, add half a wineglassful of vinegar, a little salt, pepper, and six gherkins in slices, place the cutlets in the pan to warm gently in the sauce, then dress them upon a dish, sauce over, and serve.

No. 176. *Pork Cutlets, Sauce demi Robert.* Cut eight cutlets from a neck as before, season well with pepper and salt, sprinkle chopped onions and parsley over upon both sides, beating the cutlets lightly to make them adhere, then dip them into eggs well beaten upon a plate, and then into bread-crumbs; pat them lightly, have some clarified butter in a stewpan, into which dip the cutlets, and again into bread-crumbs, well covering them, place them upon a gridiron over a moderate fire, broiling a nice light brown colour; when done dress them upon a dish. Have ready the following sauce: cut two large onions into very small dice, put them into a stewpan with an ounce of butter, fry of a light yellow colour, add a teaspoonful of flour, mix well, moisten with half a pint of broth and two spoonfuls of vinegar, season well, let boil, skim, and reduce, until rather thick, when add a spoonful of mixed mustard, one of colouring (No. 146); sauce in the centre of the cutlets and serve.

No. 177. *Hashed Pork.* Put two spoonfuls of chopped onions into a stewpan with a wineglassful of vinegar, two cloves, a blade of mace, and a bay-leaf, reduce to half, take out the spice and bay-leaf, add half a pint of broth or water, cut some pork previously cooked into thin small slices, season well upon a dish with pepper and salt, shake a good teaspoonful of flour over, mix all together, and put into the stewpan; let simmer gently ten minutes, pour out upon your dish, and serve with slices of gherkins in it; a little mustard may be added if approved of, or a little piccalilly with the vinegar is excellent.

The remains of salt pork, though very palatable cold, if required hot may be cut into large thin slices, and placed in a buttered sauté or frying-pan, with a little broth, or merely fried in the butter, and served with a puree of winter peas, made by boiling half a pint of peas until tender (tied up in a cloth); when done put them into a stewpan with two ounces of butter; season with pepper and salt, add a gill of milk or cream, pour into the dish, and dress the pork over.

No. 178. *Pig's Liver.* Procure a nice pig's liver with the caul, cut the liver into good-sized slices of the shape of hearts, season with a little pepper, salt, and cayenne, sprinkle chopped eschalots and dried sage over, and fold each piece of liver in a piece of the caul; put some butter in a sauté or frying-pan, lay them in, place over the fire, let fry rather quickly, not too dry; when done it will be a beautiful colour; take out and dress in circle upon your dish; have ready the following sauce: put six spoonfuls of melted butter in a stewpan, with one of catsup, and two of Harvey or Worcestershire sauce; when boiling pour over the liver and serve.

To plain fry it, cut in slices, season with pepper and salt, dip in flour, or eggs and bread-crumbs, fry a light brown in butter or lard, dress in a circle upon your dish, pour a gill of water into the pan, add a little Harvey sauce and a piece of butter the size of a walnut, with which you have mixed half a teaspoonful of flour; let boil a minute, add a little pepper and salt, sauce over and serve.

No. 179. *Pigs' Kidneys.* Cut them open lengthwise, season well with pepper and salt, egg over with a paste-brush, dip into bread-crumbs, with which you have mixed some chopped parsley and eschalot, run a skewer through to keep them open, and broil for about a quarter of an hour over a good fire; when done place them upon a dish, have ready an ounce of butter, with which you have mixed the juice of a lemon, a little pepper and salt, and a teaspoonful of French or common mustard, place a piece upon each of the kidneys, place in the oven for one minute and serve. Pigs' kidneys may also be sautéd as directed for ox kidneys (No. 159).

No. 180. *Black Puddings.* Very few people take the trouble to do them at home, it being part of the business of the pork butcher to prepare such delicacies. I shall, however, here describe a very simple method for making them more palatable than those purchased in England, which have so much spice in them as to entirely destroy their delicate flavour. Cut into rather small dice twenty large onions, having cut off the roots, being hard, put them into a stewpan with half a pound of lard or butter, let stew gently, cut three pounds of pig's flead, free from skin, into small dice, have ready boiled six heads of endive chopped fine, and put into the stewpan with the onions, add two ounces of salt, a saltspoonful of pepper, half a nutmeg, grated, and four spoonfuls of parsley, chopped with a little thyme and bay-leaf; then add six pints of pig's blood, mix well, leaving no lumps; if too thin add a few handfuls of bread-crumbs, or half a pound of well-boiled rice; have ready the small intestines, which well scrape and wash in salt and water, tie one end upon a tin funnel, having a piece a yard in length, closing it at the other end, fill with the above preparation by pressing through a funnel; take off the funnel, tie up the end, and put them into a stewpan of nearly boiling water, let simmer twenty minutes, pricking them occasionally with a pin; when no blood oozes out they are done; take up and place them upon a dish until cold; when ready to serve cut into pieces four inches in length, cut through the skin at different places, broil ten minutes over a sharp fire, serve plain, but very hot.

These puddings are best made whilst the blood is still warm from the pig, which if killed at home, the other ingredients may be prepared previously. The endive may be omitted, but for a real epicure procure it if possible; they are served in France on the best of tables, and are quite worthy of that honour. Many kinds of black puddings are also made in Scotland, where they more frequently use sheep's blood, using the interior of the sheep, fat and all, in the same proportions as if made of a pig, adding oatmeal, omitting part of the onions, and using the larger entrails.

It being usual in this country to introduce leeks, you must then omit the bread-crumbs and rice, or part of the onions. To prevent the blood curdling, it must be salted, by adding a handful of salt, and whisking well for ten minutes as soon as you obtain it from the pig.

Rice well boiled in broth but not too much so, is an excellent addition to black puddings (half a pound for the above quantity being quite sufficient), or grated bread; leeks also may be used instead of endive, or both may be omitted. I have mentioned these different articles, that if one cannot be procured, another might be used instead, fill also very even, mixing fat and all well together, carefully avoid letting any air get in, or they would burst in boiling.

No. 181. *Excellent Sausage Cakes.* Chop some lean pork very fine, having previously detached all the skin and bone, and to every pound of meat add three quarters of a pound of fat bacon, half an ounce of salt, a saltspoonful of pepper, the quarter of a nutmeg grated, six young green chopped onions, and a little chopped parsley; when the whole is well chopped put into a mortar and pound well, finishing with three eggs; then have ready a pig's caul, which cut into pieces large enough to fold a piece of the above preparation the size of an egg, which wrap up, keeping the shape of an egg, but rather flattened, and broil very gently over a moderate fire.

No. 182. *Pigs' Feet.* Procure six pigs' feet, nicely salted, which boil in water, to which you have added a few vegetables, until well done, cut each one in halves, take out the long bone, have some sausage meat as in the last, and a pig's caul, which cut into pieces each large enough to fold half a foot, well surrounded with sausage-meat, when well wrapped up broil slowly half an hour over a moderate fire, and serve. Or, when the pigs' feet are well boiled, egg over, and throw them into some grated crust of bread, with which you have mixed a little parsley; broil a nice colour and serve with a little plain gravy.

MADE DISHES FROM POULTRY.

No. 183. *Blanquettes of Turkey.* With the remains of a roasted or boiled turkey you may make a very nice blanquette, cutting the meat into small thin slices, chop up the bones, and put them into a stewpan with an onion, half a blade of mace, and a very little lean ham or bacon, just cover with water, boil twenty minutes, and with the stock make a white sauce as directed (No. 7, Kitchen of the Wealthy), put the slices into a stewpan, just cover with a little of the sauce, add a little white pepper, salt, and grated nutmeg, make all hot together, not, however, allowing it to boil, finish with three tablespoonfuls of cream, mixed with the yolk of an egg, stir in quickly, pour out upon a dish, and serve with triangular scippets of fried or toasted bread round. When cucumbers are in season I frequently use one, cutting it in pieces two inches in length, which again split into three, peel, and take out all the seeds, put them into a stewpan, with a few chopped onions, a little butter and sugar, and stew gently over a slow fire until tender; five minutes before serving add them to the blanquette, they being a great improvement.

No. 184. *Boudins of Turkey.* Cut up all the flesh remaining upon a turkey into small dice, if about a pound and a half, put a teaspoonful of chopped onions into a stewpan, with a piece of butter of the size of two walnuts, pass a few seconds over the fire, then add half a tablespoonful of flour (mix well) and the mince, which moisten with a pint of stock made from the bones as in the last, simmer some time, keeping it moved, season with a little pepper, salt, and sugar, finish with the yolks of three eggs, which stir in quickly over the fire, not allowing it to boil afterwards, pour out upon a dish until cold; just before ready to serve, divide it into equal parts, roll out each to about the size of small eggs, shaping them to fancy, egg and breadcrumb twice over, fry in very hot lard or dripping of a light brown colour, and serve. A little ham or tongue (should you have any left) cut small, and mixed with the mince would be a great improvement.

No. 185. *Turban of Croquettes.* Croquettes are made precisely as the last, but not more than half the size; when done, dress them in crown upon a border of mashed potatoes, and have ready some of the blanquette of turkey, which serve in the centre.

No. 186. *Minced and Grilled Turkey.* Detach the leg, wing, or take off the best part of the turkey remaining, which season well with pepper and salt, and broil over a good fire, have ready prepared a mince from the remaining flesh of the turkey, made as directed for the boudins, but omitting the yolks of eggs; when quite hot and well seasoned pour into your dish, and dress the broiled piece upon it.

No. 187. *Devilled Turkey.* Cut up the remains of your turkey into good-sized pieces or joints, if sufficient, cut incisions crosswise upon each piece, and well rub them with cayenne pepper, broil quickly over a sharp fire, dress them in your dish, and have ready the following sauce: put a tablespoonful of chopped eschalots in a stewpan with a wineglassful of Chili vinegar, reduce to half, add half a pint of thin melted butter, two tablespoonfuls of catsup, and two of Worcestershire sauce, boil about a quarter of an hour, stir in two ounces of fresh butter, pour over and serve. Many persons like the above best dry, so it would be as well to serve the sauce separate in a boat, or a little plain gravy only underneath. The remains of poulardes, capons, or fowls may be dressed precisely as directed for the turkey.

No. 188. *Goose Hashed.* The remains of a goose is only fit for hashing, or devilling, for which proceed as last directed; when for hashing put a spoonful of chopped onions into a stewpan, with an ounce of butter, pass over the fire until becoming rather brown, when add a tablespoonful of flour, mix well, cut up the remains of a goose into moderate-sized pieces, season with pepper and salt, add about a pint of stock or water, let simmer ten minutes, when pour out upon a dish and serve. For a variation, a little sage and a couple of apples sliced and cooked in the sauce is very good.

No. 189. *Stewed Duck and Peas.* Procure a duck trussed with the legs turned inside, which put into a stewpan, with two ounces of butter and a quarter of a pound of streaked bacon, let remain over a fire, stirring occasionally until lightly browned, when add a good tablespoonful of flour (mix well) and a pint of broth or water, stir round gently until boiling, when skim, and add twenty button onions, a bunch of parsley, with a bay-leaf, and two cloves, let simmer a quarter of an hour, then add a quart of nice young peas, let simmer until done, which will take about half an hour longer, take out the duck, place it upon your dish (taking away the string it was trussed with), take out the parsley and bay-leaf, season the peas with a little pepper, salt, and sugar, reduce a little if not sufficiently thick, pour over the duck and serve.

No. 190. *Duckling with Turnips* is a very favorite dish amongst the middle classes in France. Proceed as in the last, but instead of peas use about forty pieces of good turnips cut into moderate-sized square pieces, having previously fried them of a light yellow colour in a little butter or lard, and drained them upon a sieve; dress the duck upon a dish as before, season the sauce with a little pepper, salt, and sugar, reduce until rather thick, a thin sauce not suiting a dish of this description; the turnips must not, however, be in purée; sauce over and serve.

The remains of ducks left from a previous dinner may be hashed as directed for goose, and for variety, should peas be in season, a pint previously boiled may be added to the hash just before serving. The sage and apple must in all cases be omitted.

No. 191. *Fricassee of Fowl or Chicken.* Cut a fowl or chicken into eight pieces, that is, the two wings and legs dividing the back and breast into two pieces each, wash well, put them into a stewpan and cover with water, season with a teaspoonful of salt, a little pepper, a good bunch of parsley, four cloves, and a blade of mace, let boil twenty minutes, pass the stock through a sieve into a basin, take out the pieces of fowl, trim well, then in another stewpan put two ounces of butter, with which mix a good spoonful of flour, moisten with the stock, and put in the pieces of fowl, stir occasionally, until boiling, skim well, add twenty button onions, let simmer until the onions are tender, when add a gill of cream, with which you have mixed the yolks of two eggs, stir in quickly over the fire, but do not let boil, take out the pieces, dress in pyramid upon your dish, sauce over and serve.

No. 192. *Fricassee of Fowl with Mushrooms.* Proceed as in the last, but add twenty mushrooms (peeled, if very black), not too large, about ten minutes before adding the cream and yolks of eggs.

No. 193. *Currie of Fowl, Oriental Fashion.* Peel and cut two large onions into thin slices, which put into a stewpan, with two ounces of butter, fry them over a slow fire until lightly browned and quite pulpy, then add a good tablespoonful of currie-powder, and one of currie-paste, mix well, add half a pint of broth or water, let boil, keeping it stirred, then have a fowl cut into eight pieces, which put in the stewpan, cover well with the currie, add half a pint of cream, let simmer gently three quarters of an hour over a slow fire, stirring occasionally, take out the pieces, dress pyramidically upon a dish, pour the sauce over, and serve with rice plain boiled as directed (page 51) on a separate dish.

No. 194. *Broiled Fowl.* Procure a fowl trussed as for boiling, cut out the back-bone and press quite flat, season well with pepper, salt, and chopped eschalots, place in a sauté-pan, fry upon both sides, take out, egg over with a paste-brush, dip into bread-crumbs, place upon the gridiron, over a moderate fire, and broil a very light brown colour, glaze over, if any, and serve with a little plain gravy, or mushroom sauce, made by putting half a pint of melted butter into a stewpan, with about twenty button mushrooms, well washed, let simmer ten minutes, add two tablespoonfuls of catsup, and two of Harvey sauce, finish with a pat of butter, pour the sauce in the dish, dress the fowl over and serve. I very frequently also serve it at home with a sauce à la tartare made as directed page 19.

No. 195. *Fowl Sautéd in Oil.* Cut a fowl in pieces as described for the fricassee, and put them into a stewpan, with four spoonfuls of oil, place over the fire and when of a light brown colour add a good tablespoonful of flour (mix well), and moisten with a pint of broth or water, let simmer a quarter of an hour, keeping well skimmed, add a raw truffle cut in slices, or a few mushrooms, season with a little pepper, salt, sugar, and a little scraped garlic the size of a pea, take out the pieces of fowl, which dress pyramidically upon your dish, reduce the sauce over the fire, keeping it stirred until adhering to the back of the spoon, when pour over and serve.

No. 196. *Fricassee of Rabbits.* Cut two nice young rabbits into very neat joints, or the legs only may be used, and put them into lukewarm water to disgorge for half an hour, take out and put them into a stewpan with a large onion cut into slices, two cloves, a blade of mace, a little parsley, one bay-leaf, and a quarter of a pound of streaked bacon cut in dice; just cover with water, let simmer a quarter of an hour, keeping it well skimmed, pass the stock through a sieve, and proceed precisely as for the fricassee of fowl, page 689.

No. 197. *Gibelotte of Rabbits.* Cut two young rabbits into joints as in the last, cut also half a pound of streaked bacon into dice, fry the bacon in butter in a stewpan, then put in the pieces of rabbits; when slightly browned add a good spoonful of flour, mix well, and moisten with rather more than a pint of water, season with a little salt and pepper, when beginning to boil skim well, add fifty button onions, and a few button mushrooms, if any, let simmer a quarter of an hour, take out the pieces of rabbit, which dress in pyramid upon a dish; let the sauce boil, keeping it stirred, until the onions are quite tender, and the sauce thick enough to adhere to the back of the spoon, when add a little colouring, pour over the rabbit and serve.

No. 198. *Currie of Rabbit.* Cut four middling-sized onions and two apples in slices, and put them into a stewpan with two ounces of butter, place over a moderate fire, stirring occasionally, until the onions are slightly browned and quite pulpy, when add two tablespoonfuls of currie-powder and one of currie-paste; mix well, and moisten with half a pint of stock or water, let boil; have ready a couple of young rabbits cut into joints, and fried in butter in a sauté or frying-pan of a nice brown colour, put into the currie sauce, season with a little salt and juice of lemon, let stew very gently over a very slow fire, stirring occasionally, until the rabbit is quite tender, when dress upon your dish, and serve with rice, plain boiled, separate.

The legs only of the rabbits may be dressed in either of the foregoing ways, should the fillets be required for other purposes.

No. 199. *Rabbit Pies.* Cut two or three rabbits up in joints, and a pound of streaked bacon in slices; butter a pie-dish, lay some of the slices of bacon upon the bottom, dip the pieces of rabbits into flour, place a layer of them over the bacon, season well with pepper and salt, then add another layer of bacon, then rabbit, again seasoning, proceeding thus, building them in a dome above the edge of the dish; have ready a pound of half puff paste made as directed (page 480), with which cover them, ornamenting the top with leaves; egg over lightly, and bake about an hour and a half in a moderate oven, put half a pint of good gravy in with a funnel, and serve.

Rabbits plain boiled and served with onion sauce are also very excellent; make the sauce thus: peel and cut six large onions into very small dice, put into a stewpan, with two ounces of butter, pass five minutes over the fire, keeping it stirred, add two ounces of flour, mix well, moisten with a pint and a half of milk, season with a little white pepper, salt, and sugar, keep stirring over the fire until the onions are quite tender, and it becomes rather a thickish sauce, when serve over the rabbit.

The remains of rabbits may be warmed and served with the above sauce, made into blanquettes, or minced as directed for turkeys or fowls.

No. 200. *Pigeon Pie.* Procure four pigeons, but not trussed, and cut off the feet; have a nice tender rump-steak, well seasoned, which dip in flour and lay at the bottom of a buttered pie-dish; place the pigeon over, elevating their tails to meet in the centre, season well with pepper and salt, place a piece of fat bacon over the breast of each bird, sprinkle a few chopped eschalots over, have six eggs boiled, the yolks of which place in the dish, pour in half a pint of water, and cover the pie with a pound of half puff paste made as directed (page 480), ornamenting the top with leaves of paste, sticking the pigeons' feet in the centre, and brushing eggs lightly over the top; bake about an hour and a half in a moderate oven. Lamb or veal may be used instead of the beef at the bottom, if preferred, and the whole of the eggs, each cut in four lengthwise, instead of the yolks only.

No. 201. *Pigeons in Compote.* Put half a pound of lean bacon, cut into large dice, in a stewpan, with half an ounce of butter, pass a few minutes over the fire, then have three pigeons trussed with their legs turned inside, place them in the stewpan with the bacon, breasts downwards, let remain until becoming of a light brown colour, moving them round occasionally; add a tablespoonful of flour, move round until becoming a little browned, moisten with a pint, or a little more, water, mix well, add a good bunch of parsley, with a bay-leaf, thirty button onions, a little pepper and salt, let simmer three quarters of an hour, skimming well, dress the pigeons upon a dish, with the bacon and onions round, reduce the sauce to a proper consistency, take out the parsley and bay-leaf, pour over and serve.

No. 202. *Stewed Pigeons with Peas.* Proceed precisely as in the last, but adding nearly a quart of very fresh peas with the onions and parsley, omitting the bay-leaf; dress the pigeons upon a dish, pour the peas and sauce over when ready to serve.

GAME.—No. 203. *Pheasants, Partridges, Grouse, Black Game, Woodcocks, etc.*, by the greater part of the population are preferred plain roasted, which is, in my opinion, the best; but by way of change, and for the method of dressing the remains of any description of birds, I have given the few following simple receipts:

No. 204. *Small Pheasants, the Miller's Fashion.* Roast a pheasant as directed (page 403), previously dipping it in flour, and occasionally shaking flour over whilst roasting, thus it will be very crisp and keep nearly white; put the crumb of two French rolls in a stewpan, with half a pint of milk, a small eschalot, a bay-leaf, an ounce of butter, and a little pepper and salt; let boil, take out the eschalot and bay-leaf, place a piece of buttered toast upon your dish, pour the sauce over, dress the pheasant upon the top, and serve; a little gravy may also be served separate in a boat.

No. 205. *Pheasant with Cabbage.* Procure a nice white-heart winter cabbage, which cut in quarters, and blanch five minutes in boiling water, drain quite dry, cut off part of the stalk, season well with salt, place it in a stewpan, with half a pound of streaked bacon and a pint of broth, and stew gently for about half an hour; then have a pheasant about three parts roasted, thrust it into the cabbage whilst hot, and let the whole stew gently together half an hour longer; take out the pheasant and cabbage, squeezing it to the sides of the stewpan to extract the stock, dress the cabbage in pyramid upon your dish, with the pheasant upon the top, dress the bacon, cut in slices, around, skim the stock well, let reduce to half, pour round and serve.

No. 206. *Hashed Pheasant.* From the remains of a pheasant previously served, make a hash in the following manner: cut it up into smallish pieces and put them into a stewpan, with a little flour, half a glass of port wine, a little pepper and salt, and a bay-leaf, and sufficient broth (or water with a piece of glaze in it) to moisten it; let simmer very gently five minutes, take out the pieces, dress them upon your dish, pass the sauce through a hair sieve over, and serve.

No. 207. *A Plain Salmi of Pheasants.* Cut off and trim well the best pieces remaining of pheasants, previously served, and put them into a stewpan; then in another stewpan put the bones and trimmings (broken up small), with an onion in slices, a little parsley, a bay-leaf, four peppercorns, and a glass of sherry, boil a few minutes; then stir in a tablespoonful of flour, and moisten by degrees with a pint of broth (or water with a piece of glaze), boil about ten minutes, keeping it stirred; when thick enough to adhere to the back of the spoon, pass through a tammie or fine sieve, into the other stewpan over the pieces of pheasants, warm altogether gently, not allowing it to boil, colour a little brown with half a spoonful of colouring (page 673), take out the pieces, dress in pyramid sauce over, and serve with scippets of fried or toasted bread, cut in the shape of hearts, round.

The remains of pheasants may be minced and served with eggs boiled five minutes, and the shells taken off, or made into boudins or croquettes as directed for turkey (page 687), as may any other description of game.

No. 208. *Grouse, Scotch Fashion.* Plain roast the grouse, dress them upon toast on your dish, and serve with plain melted butter poured over them; they may also be dressed in any of the ways directed for pheasants, with the exception of being stewed with the cabbage; black game is dressed precisely the same as the grouse.

No. 209. *Partridges à la Jardinière.* Have a plain round tin cutter, with which cut about forty pieces of carrot and turnip, each about the thickness of a quill, and half an inch in length; put them into a stewpan with twenty button onions, two ounces of butter, and a teaspoonful of powdered sugar; pass over a sharp fire until the vegetables become covered with a thinnish glaze, when add a tablespoonful of flour (mix well) and a pint of stock or gravy; let simmer until the vegetables are tender, keeping it well skimmed. Roast two partridges rather underdone, which put into the sauce twenty minutes before serving; let simmer very gently, skim off all the fat, dress the birds upon a dish, pour the sauce and vegetables over, and serve.

No. 210. *Partridges with Cabbage.* Proceed exactly as described for the pheasant, but using two birds instead of one: if convenient, it would be a great improvement to lard the breasts of the birds with fat bacon.

No. 211. *Partridges sautéd with Mushrooms.* Divide two partridges each into halves, beat them a little flattish, put two or three tablespoonfuls of salad-oil into a flat stewpan, lay in the partridges, the inner side downwards, first seasoning with a little pepper, salt, and chopped eschalots; place over a moderate fire, put a cover upon the stewpan, and let remain until of a light brown colour; remove the lid, turn the partridges over, and let remain until coloured the other side; then pour off a little of the oil, add a tablespoonful of flour, turn round until well mixed, add a good glassful of sherry, half a pint of stock or water, and twenty small button mushrooms; let simmer until the partridges are tender, and the sauce thick enough to adhere to them; having kept it well skimmed, season with a little pepper, salt, and sugar, if required; lay the partridges upon a dish, sauce over, and serve.

The remains of partridges may be hashed or served in a plain salmi, precisely as directed for pheasants.

No. 212. *Woodcocks, Downshire Fashion.* Plain roast the woodcocks as directed (page 407), catching their tails upon toast, upon which, when done, dress the birds upon a dish; pour a thick melted butter (with which you have mixed the yolk of an egg and a little cream) over, sprinkle lightly with bread-crumbs, salamander a light brown colour, and serve with a little gravy round.

No. 213. *Woodcocks à la Chasseur.* Roast two woodcocks rather underdone, catching the interior upon a large piece of toast; when done, cut each one in four, and place in a stewpan with the remainder of the interior, chopped small; add a little pepper and salt, a glass of sherry, a little chopped eschalots, parsley, the juice of half a lemon, and half a gill of broth; let simmer a few minutes, dish rather high upon the toast, sauce over, and serve.

No. 214. *Hashed Woodcocks.* Should you have any remaining from a previous dinner, cut each one in four or more pieces; chop all that remains in the interior, which mix with a small piece of butter, a spoonful of bread-crumbs, and a little chopped parsley, make six croutons in the shape of hearts from a piece of toasted bread, spread the above preparation upon each, and place a short time in the oven; hash the pieces as directed for the pheasant, dress in pyramid on a dish, with the croutons round, sauce over, and serve.

No. 215. *Snipes à la Minute.* Put a quarter of a pound of butter in a stewpan, over which lay six snipes, breasts downwards; add a spoonful of chopped onions, one ditto of parsley, a little grated nutmeg, half a teaspoonful of salt, and a saltspoonful of pepper; set over a brisk fire seven or ten minutes (according to the size of the birds), stirring occasionally, then add the juice of two lemons, two glasses of sherry or bucellas wine, and a spoonful of finely-grated crust of bread; let the whole simmer a few minutes, dress the birds upon a dish, mix the sauce well, pour over, and serve.

No. 216. *Plovers, with English raw Truffles.* Put a quarter of a pound of butter in a stewpan, over which place four plovers, breasts downwards, and eight raw truffles, well washed, peeled, and cut into thickish slices; add also two cloves, a bay-leaf, half a teaspoonful of salt, and a saltspoonful of pepper; pass the whole ten minutes over a sharp fire, stirring occasionally; add half a tablespoonful of flour, mix well, moisten with a gill of broth and a glass of white wine, let simmer ten minutes longer, skim well, dress the birds upon a dish, reduce the sauce, add a little sugar and the juice of a lemon, sauce over, and serve.

No. 217. *Wild Duck.* Truss as directed (p. 688, No. 189), rub all over with the liver, making it quite red, and roast twenty minutes before a good fire, then with a sharp knife cut eight incisions down the breast; you have put an ounce of butter into a stewpan with a quarter of a saltspoonful of cayenne, the rind of an orange, free from pith, cut in strips, blanched in boiling water, and well drained upon a sieve, and the juice of a lemon; warm over the fire, and when melted, but not oily, pour over the duck, and serve.

No. 218. *Hashed Wild Duck.* Cut up the remains of a duck or ducks into neat pieces, and put into a stewpan with half or a tablespoonful of flour, depending upon the quantity; mix well, moisten with a glass or two of wine, and sufficient broth or water to make a thickish sauce, season well, add a little Harvey sauce, mushroom catsup, a little sugar, and cayenne pepper; let simmer but not boil, take out the pieces, which dress upon toast, reduce the sauce, pour over, and serve. A little colouring may be added if approved of.

No. 219. *Widgeons.* Truss as for wild ducks, rub over with some of their livers, chop up the remainder, which mix with a few bread-crumbs, a little chopped lemon-peel, chopped parsley, and an egg, with which stuff the interior; roast nearly as long as for the wild duck before a very sharp fire, dress upon toast on a dish, and have ready the following sauce: put half a glass of port wine into a stewpan, with a teaspoonful of chopped eschalot, a little salt, pepper, and cayenne; boil a few minutes, add the juice of a lemon, and two ounces of fresh butter, sauce over, and serve. Widgeons are hashed in the same manner as described for wild duck.

No. 220. *Teal, a new Method.* Procure four, draw them, then put half a pound of butter upon a plate, with a little pepper, grated nutmeg, parsley, a spoonful of grated crust of bread, the juice of a lemon, and the liver of the teal; mix well together, and with it fill the interior of the teal; cover them with slices of lemon, fold in thin slices of bacon, then in paper, and roast twenty minutes before a sharp fire; take off the paper, brown the bacon, dress them upon a slice of thick toast, letting the butter from the teal run over it, and serve very hot.

No. 221. *Teal à la sans Façon.* Roast four teal quite plain, prepare a quarter of a pound of butter, as above, with the omission of the livers, which place in a stewpan over the fire, stirring quickly, until forming a kind of sauce; add some fillets from the pulp of a lemon, sauce over, and serve. The remains of teal also make an excellent hash.

No. 222. *Larks à la Minute.* Proceed as directed for snipes à la minute, previously stuffing them with their livers, as directed for widgeons, adding a few mushrooms at the commencement, and not letting them stew too quickly, or the bottom would become brown and give a bad flavour to the sauce; ten minutes is quite sufficient to stew them.

No. 223. *Lark Pie.* Cover the bottom of a pie-dish with thin slices of beef and fat bacon, over which lay ten or twelve larks, previously rolled in flour, season with a teaspoonful of salt, a quarter do. of pepper, one of chopped parsley, and one of chopped eschalot; lay a bay-leaf over, add a gill of broth, and cover with three quarters of a pound of half puff paste (p. 480); bake one hour in a moderate oven, shake well to make the gravy in the pie form a kind of sauce, and serve quite hot.

No. 224. *Jugged Hare.* Put nearly half a pound of butter into a good-sized stewpan with ten ounces of flour, making rather a thinnish roux by continually turning over a slow fire until becoming of a yellowish tinge, then add a pound of good streaked bacon, previously cut into good-sized square pieces; keep stirring a few minutes longer over the fire; you have previously cut the hare into nice pieces, throw them into the stewpan, and stir over the fire until becoming firm, when moisten with four glasses of port wine, and sufficient water to cover them; when beginning to boil, skim well, season in proportion to the size of your hare, let simmer, add two bay-leaves, four cloves, and, when about half done, forty button onions, or ten large ones, cut into slices; let simmer until the whole is well done, the sauce requiring to be rather thick; dress the pieces as high as possible upon your dish, sauce over, and serve. The remains are excellent either cold or warmed up again in the stewpan. If cheap and in season, a few small new potatoes are excellent stewed with it.

No. 225. *Another and more simple Method.* Put a quarter of a pound of butter with a pound of bacon, cut into dice, and the hare, cut into pieces, in a stewpan set upon a moderate fire until the pieces of hare are becoming firm, when add six ounces of flour, mix well and moisten with sufficient water to cover it, add two glasses of any kind of wine and one of vinegar, season as above, let simmer until tender, keeping well skimmed: when done, and the sauce becoming quite thick, dress upon your dish, and serve as before.

www.ingramcontent.com/pod-product-compliance
Lightning Source LLC
Chambersburg PA
CBHW081729100526
44591CB00016B/2556